THE ULTIMATE
DENVER BRONCOS
TRIVIA BOOK

A Collection of Amazing Trivia Quizzes and Fun Facts for Die-Hard Broncos Fans!

Ray Walker

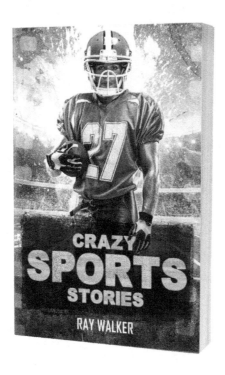

CONTENTS

INTRODUCTION

The first few years were tough on the Denver Broncos but, over the last 35 years, the Broncos have become one of the best teams in football. John Elway turned three heartbreaks in four years into consecutive years of joy at the end of his career in 1997 and 1998. Peyton Manning had a career revival in the Mile High City and led Denver back to the top of the NFL world in 2015. In between, there were plenty of highs and lows with a variety of success but the Broncos were no longer at the bottom of the league.

Denver hasn't had the same star power as some of the other franchises in the league, but still some of the best players wore the blue and orange. Quarterbacks like Elway and Manning highlight that list, along with running back Terrell Davis and tight end Shannon Sharpe, two of the premier players at their positions. Then there are the modern-day stars, like linebacker Von Miller, who are on the path to one day have their busts enshrined in Canton, Ohio.

This book is designed to test the most die-hard Broncos fans with trivia that will test even the biggest of fans. Each of the 12 chapters in this book focuses on a specific topic from the history of the franchise to specific positions to the record book. Each chapter features 20 multiple-choice or true-false questions, followed by the answers to those questions and then 10 facts about the chapter topic that shed light on a random part of Broncos history. Do not be alarmed if some of these questions stump you; the point is to help you learn more about your favorite team.

We hope you learn something new after devouring this book and use it to show off to your fellow Broncos fans. All of these facts and figures are current as of the beginning of the 2020 season, so keep that in mind when reading and answering the questions. Now all that's left is to sit back, relax, and enjoy the hours of fun this book provides for the biggest and baddest Denver Broncos fans in the world.

CHAPTER 1:

ORIGINS & HISTORY

QUIZ TIME!

1. What was the nickname given to Bob Howsam and the other seven owners who bought into the American Football League?

    a. American Hero Brigade
    b. Einstein Eight
    c. Silly Brigade
    d. Foolish Club

2. How many seats were being added to Bears Stadium when Howsam brought the Broncos to Denver?

    a. 8,000
    b. 9,000
    c. 10,000
    d. 12,000

3. Sharing a baseball stadium with a baseball team became problematic, so where did the Broncos end up playing some of their early-season home games?

a. Folsom Field

b. Hilltop Stadium

c. Colorado Field

d. They opened every year with road games until baseball season ended

4. Which AFC West rival was Denver's opponent for its first home game in 1960?

a. Oakland Raiders

b. Kansas City Chiefs

c. San Diego Chargers

d. Seattle Seahawks

5. After winning three of their first four games in the AFL, the Broncos struggled in the second half of the season. How many consecutive games did Denver go winless to end the inaugural 1960 season?

a. 6

b. 7

c. 8

d. 9

6. The Broncos' first coach and starting quarterback both came from which team in the Canadian Football League?

a. Toronto Argonauts

b. Saskatchewan Roughriders

c. Hamilton Tiger-Cats

d. Edmonton Eskimos

7. What color were Denver's original uniforms, which quarterback Frank Tripucka called "the ugliest-looking things you ever wanted to see"?

    a. Green and black
    b. Gold and silver
    c. Orange and purple
    d. Mustard and brown

8. Denver went unbeaten against both the Boston Patriots and Buffalo Bills in its inaugural season.

    a. True
    b. False

9. Which AFL Coach of the Year did Frank Tripucka call "an organizer" and cite as a reason why Denver's fortunes turned around so quickly in 1962?

    a. Jack Faulkner
    b. Frank Filchock
    c. Mac Speedie
    d. Ray Malavasi

10. In which season did the Denver lose its opening game of the season for the first time in franchise history?

    a. 1961
    b. 1962
    c. 1963
    d. 1964

11. Which one of these quarterbacks did not throw at least 15 passes for the Broncos during the 1963 season?

a. Don Breaux

b. George Shaw

c. John McCormick

d. Frank Tripucka

12. Which quarterback did Denver trade for from the Houston Oilers in 1964 on the condition it would return him to Houston before the 1966 season?

a. Jacky Lee

b. Mickey Slaughter

c. John McCormick

d. Lance Leasee

13. Which city presented an enticing offer to lure the Broncos out of Denver in 1965 amid fledgling attendance and ticket sales?

a. Seattle

b. Atlanta

c. Tampa Bay

d. Phoenix

14. When did the Broncos finally have their first winning season?

a. 1969

b. 1971

c. 1973

d. 1975

15. Who was Denver's opponent in the first-ever NFL regular-season game to go into overtime?

a. Kansas City Chiefs

b. Miami Dolphins

c. Cleveland Browns

d. Pittsburgh Steelers

16. What was the nickname of the famous defense that led the Broncos to their first Super Bowl appearance after the 1977 season?

a. Clockwork Orange

b. Orange Crush

c. Orange Express

d. Orange Juice

17. The Broncos have faced eight different opponents in their eight Super Bowl appearances.

a. True

b. False

18. How many different coaches have led the Broncos to the playoffs?

a. 4

b. 5

c. 6

d. 7

19. Which Denver head coach never was a coordinator for the Broncos before ascending to the top job?

a. Wade Phillips

b. Mike Shanahan

c. Red Miller

d. Gary Kubiak

20. Which team has been the Broncos' most frequent opponent in the playoffs?

a. Miami Dolphins
b. Pittsburgh Steelers
c. New England Patriots
d. Oakland Raiders

QUIZ ANSWERS

1. D – Foolish Club

2. A – 8,000

3. B – Hilltop Stadium

4. A – Oakland Raiders

5. C – 5

6. B – Saskatchewan Roughriders

7. D – Mustard and Brown

8. A – True

9. A – Jack Faulkner

10. C – 1963

11. B – George Shaw

12. A – Jacky Lee

13. B – Atlanta

14. C – 1973

15. D – Pittsburgh Steelers

16. B – Orange Crush

17. A – True

18. C – 6

19. C – Red Miller

20. B – Pittsburgh Steelers

DID YOU KNOW?

1. The Denver Broncos were close to never actually existing
    in the first place. Bob Howsam had plans to buy into the
    Continental League, a third-tier professional baseball
    league, and set up a franchise in Denver. However, Major
    League Baseball added the Houston Astros as an
    expansion team, relocated the Washington Senators to
    Minnesota, and brought National League baseball back to
    New York with the expansion Mets. Those changes
    precipitated the death of the Continental League before it
    got off the ground and Howsam joined the "Foolish Club"
    to bring the American Football League to Denver.

2. The Broncos were at a major disadvantage compared to
    their competitors in the AFL. Most of the owners in the
    league were businessmen who had success in other
    ventures and could have far bigger budgets than what
    Howsam allotted the Broncos. Howsam was in the sports
    business, so he only allowed the franchise to spend what
    it brought in in revenue. The team's budget was so small
    that its first uniforms with the memorable striped socks
    were actually hand-me-downs from the Copper Bowl.

3. When Jack Faulkner took over as the Broncos coach in
    1962, he brought about several changes to make the team
    more professional. Denver's practices actually featured
    tackling, the coach enforced a curfew, and he installed a

dress code of coats and ties for road trips. Faulkner also barred his players from smoking in public. He created an organizational structure that allowed his players to flourish. The Broncos opened the season 7-2 and led the Western Division before crashing with five straight losses to miss out on the championship game.

4. The 1963 season opener against the newly-renamed Kansas City Chiefs still stands as the worst home loss in franchise history. The Chiefs shellacked the Broncos 59-7 as Denver put up only 181 yards of total offense in the humiliating defeat. Len Dawson threw 4 touchdown passes for Kansas City while Denver's Mickey Slaughter had a pass intercepted and returned for a touchdown. The Broncos tumbled to a 2-11-1 record that season, which ended with nine losses and a tie in the final 10 games.

5. The deal to bring Jacky Lee to Denver was certainly an odd one. The Broncos shipped all-league defensive tackle Bud McFadin, a draft pick, and some cash to Houston for the right to effectively rent Lee for two seasons. Lee's nickname became "Lend-Lease Lee," and it only further enhanced the views outsiders had about the Denver franchise. Lee wasn't going to play in Houston with George Blanda on the roster, so the Oilers sent him to the Broncos to get some experience, treating their league rival like a farm team for talent within a league seen as the minor leagues to the NFL. Faulkner was Lee's position coach at the University of Cincinnati, but Lee didn't match his college production in Denver, throwing almost

twice as many interceptions (20) as touchdowns (11) in the disastrous 1964 campaign.

6. The threat that the Broncos might leave for Atlanta was the wake-up call Denver needed to support its football team. After the Phipps brothers announced that they had bought a controlling interest in the team on February 16, 1965, and rejected Atlanta's offer, the team set out to sell 20,000 season tickets. By April, the Broncos hit that goal and the final tally exceeded 23,000 season tickets sold. The sales drive vaulted Denver from last in the league in attendance to fourth at nearly 31,400 fans per game.

7. Ties have played a strange part in the Denver Broncos' history. The Broncos and Raiders played to a 23-23 tie in Denver's first Monday Night Football appearance on October 22, 1973. Jim Turner's 35-yard field goal – his third of the game – tied the game and extended the Broncos' unbeaten run that would last a then-record eight games. The following season, Denver and Pittsburgh met in Denver and played the first regular-season game to go into overtime. That game also ended in a tie despite Denver holding a 21-7 lead over the defending Super Bowl champions after the first quarter.

8. The 1977 Denver Broncos captured the hearts of thousands of fans around Colorado as the Orange Crush defense helped the Broncos bulldoze their way to the Super Bowl. It was the first time the Broncos had ever appeared in the playoffs and they made the most of their

opportunity with a pair of holiday triumphs to reach New Orleans for the Super Bowl. In the divisional round, Denver defeated Pittsburgh on Christmas Eve to deny the Steelers a chance at a third Super Bowl in four years. On New Year's Day, the Broncos avenged their first loss of the season by beating the Raiders in the AFC Championship Game, thus denying their rivals a return trip to the Super Bowl. The run ended against Dallas in the Super Bowl, but after the game ended, the Cowboys' celebration was dampened by tens of thousands of Broncos fans chanting "We love You" at the team as it left the field.

9. The Broncos are one of five teams to play in at least seven Super Bowls, but they are the only team to have a losing record in those appearances. Denver lost four Super Bowls before finally winning back-to-back titles following the 1997 and 1998 seasons then split their two appearances this century with Peyton Manning at the helm. Only the New England Patriots have lost as many Super Bowls as the Broncos' five defeats, but the Patriots also have six victories compared to just three for the Broncos.

10. The future of the Denver Broncos is currently up in the air due to an ongoing legal battle surrounding the estate of late owner Pat Bowlen, who bought the team in 1984 and died in June 2019. His two oldest children are suing to invalidate the trust Bowlen formed in 2009 on the grounds he was not mentally capable of making decisions due to effects from Alzheimer's Disease. Joe Ellis has been

running the franchise's day-to-day operations as its president and CEO since 2013, when Bowlen notified the NFL of his decision to step away from operations due to his disease.

CHAPTER 2:

NUMBERS GAME

QUIZ TIME!

1. The Denver Broncos have had someone wear all 100 legal numbers.

    a. True
    b. False

2. Which jersey number is the only one to be worn by two different Hall-of-Famers with the Broncos?

    a. 7
    b. 24
    c. 30
    d. 80

3. Which two players wore No. 44 before Floyd Little arrived in Denver in 1967?

    a. Don Allen and Pete Mangum
    b. Bruce Starling and Miller Farr
    c. Lew Scott and Chuck Marshall
    d. Justin Rowland and Al Frazier

4. Which one of these quarterbacks never wore No. 15 for the Broncos?

   a. Jacky Lee
   b. Tim Tebow
   c. Marlin Briscoe
   d. Danny Kanell

5. How many jersey numbers have the Broncos officially retired?

   a. 2
   b. 3
   c. 4
   d. 6

6. Peyton Manning is the only quarterback to start a Super Bowl for Denver who didn't wear the No. 7.

   a. True
   b. False

7. Which number did legendary linebacker Tom Jackson make famous during his tenure with the Orange Crush?

   a. 45
   b. 50
   c. 56
   d. 57

8. Because Champ Bailey was already wearing No. 24, Ty Law had to pick a new number when he signed with the Broncos in 2009. Which one did Law wear in his seven games with Denver?

a. 23

b. 25

c. 26

d. 28

9. Before his resurgence in the early 2000s, Tommy Maddox was a first-round draft choice of the Broncos. Which number did he wear during his short career in Denver?

a. 4

b. 6

c. 8

d. 10

10. Which Denver first-round pick wore No. 30 before Terrell Davis tore up the league wearing that number for the Broncos?

a. Alton Montgomery

b. Steve Sewell

c. Gerald Willhite

d. Tony Lilly

11. Which current NFL quarterback credits John Elway as the reason he wears the No. 7?

a. Ben Roethlisberger

b. Mike Glennon

c. Dwayne Haskins

d. Taysom Hill

12. Who was the first player to wear the No. 99 for multiple seasons in Denver?

a. Vonnie Holliday

b. Ray Woodard

c. Shane Dronett

d. Montae Reagor

13. The No. 13 isn't unlucky for this Northwestern quarterback who brought his college number to Denver as a seventh-round draft pick.

    a. Steve Tensi

    b. Mike Kafka

    c. Craig Penrose

    d. Trevor Siemian

14. Which number did 1988's First Team All-Pro punter Mike Horan wear for the Broncos?

    a. 2

    b. 3

    c. 5

    d. 7

15. The only Denver Broncos to wear No. 1 for the team were kickers and punters.

    a. True

    b. False

16. Forty-two might be the answer to life, but it's also the number worn by Casey Kreiter the last four seasons in Denver. What position does Kreiter play?

    a. Linebacker

    b. Safety

c. Offensive guard

d. Long snapper

17. For 12 seasons, Shannon Sharpe made the No. 84 famous as the best tight end in the NFL. Which player did not wear that number for the Broncos after Sharpe retired?

a. Brandon Lloyd

b. Jacob Tamme

c. Javon Walker

d. Wes Welker

18. No Denver player has worn the No. 65 since Gary Zimmerman was elected into the Pro Football Hall of Fame in 2008.

a. True

b. False

19. For 10 seasons, Steve Atwater terrified opposing offenses while roaming the field in what number?

a. 17

b. 27

c. 37

d. 47

20. In 2019, Drew Lock became the first quarterback in franchise history to wear No. 3. Which kicker made the number famous by wearing it in two Super Bowls for Denver?

a. Jason Elam

b. Matt Prater

c. Rich Karlis

d. Connor Barth

QUIZ ANSWERS

1. A – True

2. B – 24

3. B – Bruce Starling and Miller Farr

4. D – Danny Kanell

5. B – 3

6. A – True

7. D – 57

8. C – 26

9. C – 8

10. B – Steve Sewell

11. A – Ben Roethlisberger

12. C – Shane Dronett

13. D – Trevor Siemian

14. A – 2

15. A – True

16. D – Long Snapper

17. D – Wes Welker

18. B – False

19. B – 27

20. C – Rich Karlis

DID YOU KNOW?

1. In 1962, fullback John Olszewski became the first and only member of the Broncos to wear No. 0 when he donned the number. He was a prolific fullback in the 1950s and ended his career with the Broncos for two seasons. He earned his nickname, "Johnny O," both due to his last name and the number he wore at two different stops before Denver as well.

2. The No. 18 was the first jersey to be retired by the Broncos franchise and it was also the most recently used number of the three that have been retired. When Frank Tripucka retired midway through the 1963 season, the team held a midfield ceremony to honor its first quarterback. Owner Cal Kunz announced at that moment that no one else would ever wear the No. 18 for the Broncos again. Almost 50 years later, Tripucka agreed to let Peyton Manning wear No. 18 when he signed with Denver, so they are the only two players ever to wear the number for the Broncos in their history.

3. Von Miller might have been considering switching his number from his now-iconic 58 to 40, which he wore at Texas A&M. In June 2020, Miller posted a poll on Twitter asking if he should keep wearing No. 58 or change to No. 40; keeping his No. 58 won the vote with 73.5 percent. Miller originally wanted to wear 40 when he entered the

league but linebackers were not allowed to wear numbers in the 40s when he was drafted. He chose 58 to honor Derrick Thomas, but now he could change back to No. 40, and he might just be considering it.

4. Demaryius Thomas has a very simple explanation behind wearing No. 88 for Denver. He told the team website, "When I first got here I went in to see 'Flip' [Chris Valenti], our equipment manager. And he was like, well, the last time the Broncos won the Super Bowl, somebody had the number 88. So, I was like, 'Cool, give it to me.'" One can never doubt the power of superstition in the sports world.

5. When Champ Bailey was inducted into the Pro Football Hall of Fame in 2019, he became the second Hall-of-Famer to have worn No. 24 for the Broncos. He sported that number for all 10 seasons he played in Denver, joining Willie Brown, who wore the number in his first four seasons in the NFL, as a Hall-of-Famer.

6. The first six times Denver played in the Super Bowl, a quarterback wearing No. 7 was under center for the Broncos. The first time Denver earned a spot in the championship game was 1977, when Craig Morton led the offense at quarterback. The next five Super Bowls were quarterbacked by the legendary John Elway. Peyton Manning wore No. 18 for both of his appearances in the Super Bowl with Denver.

7. Bronco great Floyd Little is part of the exclusive fraternity of Syracuse football players who wore No. 44 while

playing for the Orange. His No. 44 is also retired by the Broncos, but he said in 2015 that he's willing to unretire the number if his grandson, Blaze, plays at Syracuse. Little gave Blaze the helmet and jersey he received in 2005 when Syracuse officially retired the number but cautioned that Blaze won't be able to wear the number if he ends up being a lineman.

8. Before becoming the head coach of the Los Angeles Chargers, Anthony Lynn was a backup running back for six seasons in the NFL. He spent four of those years with the Broncos and wore No. 37 in 61 appearances. Another former head coach who played in Denver was Gary Kubiak, who wore No. 8 for the Broncos during his playing days.

9. It took five years for someone to work up the courage to wear the No. 80 after Rod Smith retired after the 2006 season. But tight end Julius Thomas did the number proud in 2013 and 2014, his third and fourth years with the number. He caught 12 touchdowns in both seasons to help Denver make the playoffs.

10. CBS Sports released a list in July 2020 listing the best players for each jersey number in NFL history. Nine of the 100 players listed played at some point for the Broncos in their careers. Several famous Broncos were easily picked for the list: John Elway for No. 7, Peyton Manning for No. 18, and Steve Atwater for No. 27. Champ Bailey was selected as the best to wear No. 24, Terrell Davis took

home the honor for No. 30, Dennis Smith for No. 49, and DeMarcus Ware for No. 94. Jay Cutler was named the best No. 6 in league history and Tony Dorsett was the best No. 33 to round out the Broncos' representation.

CHAPTER 3:

HAIL TO ALMA MATER

QUIZ TIME!

1. From which school have the Denver Broncos drafted the most players?

   a. LSU

   b. Alabama

   c. Georgia

   d. Florida

2. Demaryius Thomas starred as a receiver for which run-happy college football team?

   a. Georgia Tech

   b. The Citadel

   c. Georgia Southern

   d. Coastal Carolina

3. Shannon Sharpe was a three-time All-American and three-time conference offensive player of the year at which Division II school?

   a. Clark-Atlanta University

   b. Savannah State

c. Kennesaw State

d. South Carolina State

4. The Broncos have historically had a lot of success with running backs from the University of Georgia. Which of these Denver running backs did not play for the Bulldogs?

a. Tatum Bell

b. Knowshon Moreno

c. Terrell Davis

d. Garrison Hearst

5. For seven years, John Mobley roamed the field as a linebacker for Denver after plying his trade at which Division II school?

a. Kutztown

b. Lock Haven

c. Slippery Rock

d. Millersville

6. Broncos coach Vic Fangio played football at East Stroudsburg University and it was his college coach, Denny Douds, who inspired him to become a coach instead of pursuing a professional playing career.

a. True

b. False

7. At which school did two-time First Team All-Pro and four-time Pro Bowl tackle Ryan Clady play college football before becoming Denver's 2008 first-round pick?

a. Texas Christian

b. Oregon

c. Oklahoma

d. Boise State

8. Brandon Marshall had three 1,000-yard seasons as a receiver after the Broncos drafted him out of which school?

a. Miami

b. South Florida

c. Central Florida

d. Auburn

9. Jason Elam is the Broncos all-time leading scorer. Where did the kicker play college football?

a. Washington State

b. San Diego State

c. Hawaii

d. Fresno State

10. At which Big Ten school did Eric Decker cement his mark when he left as the program's all-time leading receiver?

a. Wisconsin

b. Minnesota

c. Iowa

d. Purdue

11. Despite drafting only 15 players from the University of Colorado, the Broncos have had 34 former Buffaloes on the roster, more than any other college.

a. True

b. False

12. Who was the last player from the University of Colorado that the Denver Broncos drafted?

    a. Ty Sambrailo
    b. Juwann Winfree
    c. Phillip Lindsay
    d. Virgil Green

13. According to the Broncos, how many players have they had who never attended college?

    a. 4
    b. 5
    c. 6
    d. 7

14. Bradley Chubb holds the record for most sacks by a rookie after Denver drafted him in the first round out of which ACC school?

    a. North Carolina State
    b. North Carolina
    c. Wake Forest
    d. Duke

15. Before patrolling the field with the Broncos, where did Simon Fletcher play college football?

    a. Houston
    b. Baylor
    c. Texas Christian
    d. Texas A&M

16. Lou Saban dipped his toe into coaching college football for the first time after being fired by the Broncos.

    a. True
    b. False

17. Craig Morton led the Broncos to their first Super Bowl, but before then he set almost every school record as a three-year starter at which Pac-12 school?

    a. Washington
    b. Stanford
    c. UCLA
    d. California

18. Before Rod Smith made fans in Denver very happy as an undrafted free agent, he starred at which Division II school?

    a. Pittsburg State
    b. Missouri Western
    c. Missouri Southern State
    d. Central Oklahoma

19. Tom Nalen spent 15 years in the middle of the Broncos offensive line after Denver drafted him out of which New England school?

    a. Connecticut
    b. New Hampshire
    c. Boston College
    d. Massachusetts

20. In 1997, the Broncos had only three draft picks: Trevor Pryce, Dan Neil, and Cory Gilliard. Each went to a different school; which school is the odd one out?

a. Clemson
b. Ball State
c. LSU
d. Texas

QUIZ ANSWERS

1. D – Florida

2. A – Georgia Tech

3. B – Savannah State

4. A – Tatum Bell

5. A – Kutztown

6. B – False

7. D – Boise State

8. C – Central Florida

9. C – Hawaii

10. B – Minnesota

11. A – True

12. B – Juwann Winfree

13. D – 7

14. A – North Carolina State

15. A – Houston

16. B – False

17. D – California

18. C – Missouri Southern State

19. C – Boston College

20. C – LSU

DID YOU KNOW?

1. The Broncos have found some good players from smaller schools. In addition to Mobley and Sharpe hailing from smaller schools, longtime starting defensive back Tyrone Braxton played at North Dakota State, defensive end Barney Chavous went to school at South Carolina State, Todd Davis played at Sacramento State, and running back Fran Lynch played at Hofstra.

2. There have been plenty of other players from small schools who have made the Broncos roster in the last 60 years. Among the schools represented by Denver players are Adams State, American International College, Elizabeth City State, McMurray College, Saginaw Valley State, and Yankton College.

3. Mark Schlereth might be the best-known Alaskan football player, but it was a long road from Anchorage to the NFL. He never was an all-state player and his high school team went 1-6 during his senior year. He ended up going to the University of Idaho, a Division I-AA (now FCS) school, and anchored the offensive line to three Big Sky Conference titles. During his senior year, the Vandals advanced all the way to the national semifinals and Schlereth earned second-team All-American honors.

4. Phillip Lindsay was a steal as an undrafted free agent out of Colorado, considering that the running back's name is

all over the record book in Boulder. He ranks second in career rushing with 3,707 yards and 36 touchdowns and he ranks fourth all-time in scoring with 234 points. He leads the Buffaloes in all-purpose yards (5,760) and yards from scrimmage (4,683).

5. Not only has Colorado put the most players on the Broncos, but those players have also played the most combined game for the franchise. Former Buffaloes have played 1,208 games for Denver, almost 400 more than the 840 games played by the 24 former Georgia Bulldogs. John Elway accounts for exactly one-third of the games played by the 23 Stanford alumni to have suited up for the Broncos.

6. Before breaking barriers as the first black starting quarterback in professional football, Marlin Briscoe was dominating the competition at Omaha University – now the University of Nebraska-Omaha. He left the school with 22 school records as he led the team to three conference championships. Among the records he set are most touchdown passes (52), passing yards (4,935), and total offense (6,253 yards).

7. We can't really talk about college careers for former Broncos and not talk about Tim Tebow. A two-time national champion, Tebow became the first sophomore to ever win the Heisman Trophy in 2007 and finished in the top five in each of the next two seasons. Although he was not the traditional quarterback by any stretch, Tebow still

33

completed 66.4 percent of his passes in his four years at Florida, tossing 88 touchdowns to just 16 interceptions in that span. He added 57 rushing touchdowns and 2,947 rushing yards. He is tied for the FBS record with 38 games in which he scored a touchdown.

8. Tebow is one of three former Heisman winners to suit up for the Broncos and also the longest-tenured. He lasted two seasons in Denver, which is longer than 1999 winner Ron Dayne and 1982 Heisman recipient Tony Dorsett. Dayne appeared in 10 games for the Broncos in 2005, rushing 53 times for 270 yards. Dorsett finished his Hall of Fame career with Denver in 1988 and started 13 games for the Broncos.

9. Denver's first starting quarterback had to wait a while to earn his chance at Notre Dame during his college career. Frank Tripucka was a three-year letter winner for the Fighting Irish but was the backup behind 1947 Heisman-winning quarterback John Lujack for his first three seasons. He finally had a chance to lead Notre Dame in 1948 and his played helped the Fighting Irish finish 9-0-1 this season. During his career in South Bend, Tripucka completed 80 of 141 passes for 1,122 yards and 14 touchdowns with just one interception.

10. As if Rod Smith wasn't impressive enough on the field, he made it count in the classroom as well as Missouri Southern State University. Smith earned three degrees – economics and finance; general business; and marketing

and management – while setting 11 school records playing football for the Lions. He was the school's "Outstanding Graduate" in 1993 and he was also a member of the school's basketball team in 1990-91.

CHAPTER 4:

CALLING THE SIGNALS

QUIZ TIME!

1. How many yards did Frank Tripucka throw for during the Broncos' inaugural season?

    a. 2,762

    b. 2,874

    c. 3,038

    d. 3,196

2. Eight different quarterbacks led the Broncos in passing yards from 1963-1971. Who was the only quarterback to do it twice in that span?

    a. Mickey Slaughter

    b. Steve Tensi

    c. Pete Liske

    d. John McCormick

3. Marlin Briscoe threw more touchdowns than interceptions in his one year as the Denver starter.

    a. True

    b. False

4. How many wins did Craig Morton have as the Broncos' starting quarterback?

   a. 35
   b. 37
   c. 39
   d. 41

5. Which quarterback acquired from San Francisco was thrust into the spotlight in 1982 to replace the aging Craig Morton?

   a. Mark Herrmann
   b. Steve DeBerg
   c. Gary Kubiak
   d. Matt Robinson

6. How many yards did John Elway's famous drive cover against the Cleveland Browns in the 1986 AFC Championship Game?

   a. 96
   b. 97
   c. 98
   d. 99

7. What percentage of Denver's points was John Elway directly responsible for by either passing, rushing, or receiving during his 16-year career?

   a. 81.1
   b. 82.2
   c. 83.3
   d. 84.4

8. How many times did John Elway pass for at least 3,000 yards in a season?

    a. 10
    b. 11
    c. 12
    d. 13

9. John Elway threw for 300 yards against the same opponent in consecutive weeks.

    a. True
    b. False

10. How many game-winning or game-tying drives did John Elway orchestrate in the fourth quarter during his career?

    a. 34
    b. 38
    c. 43
    d. 47

11. Brian Griese started all 16 games during the 1999 season, Denver's first since John Elway retired.

    a. True
    b. False

12. How many different quarterbacks have led the Broncos in passing yards in a season since John Elway retired?

    a. 6
    b. 7
    c. 8
    d. 9

13. From which team did the Broncos lure quarterback Jake Plummer during free agency in 2003?

    a. Arizona Cardinals
    b. Seattle Seahawks
    c. San Diego Chargers
    d. Tampa Bay Buccaneers

14. Who is the only other Denver quarterback aside from Peyton Manning to pass for 4,500 yards in a season?

    a. Jay Cutler
    b. Kyle Orton
    c. John Elway
    d. Jake Plummer

15. Tim Tebow might be most known in Denver for his 80-yard game-winning touchdown pass in the 2011 AFC Wild Card Game. How many passes did he complete in that game?

    a. 9
    b. 10
    c. 11
    d. 12

16. What was Tim Tebow's career regular-season completion percentage in his 23 games for the Broncos?

    a. 46.5
    b. 47.3
    c. 48.2
    d. 49.7

17. What type of injury did Peyton Manning sustain that opened the door for his move to Denver in 2012?

    a. Knee
    b. Head
    c. Neck
    d. Back

18. Which award did Peyton Manning not win during his time with the Broncos?

    a. All-NFL First Team
    b. Most Valuable Player
    c. Comeback Player of the Year
    d. Super Bowl MVP

19. In how many consecutive games did Peyton Manning throw a touchdown pass for the Broncos?

    a. 44
    b. 40
    c. 38
    d. 33

20. Trevor Siemian was Denver's seventh-round draft pick out of Northwestern in 2015 and he started 24 games in 2016 and 2017. Who was the first-round quarterback that Siemian beat out for the job in both seasons?

    a. Blake Bortles
    b. Sean Mannion
    c. Paxton Lynch
    d. Johnny Manziel

QUIZ ANSWERS

1. C – 3,038

2. B – Steve Tensi

3. A – True

4. D – 41

5. B – Steve DeBerg

6. C – 98

7. B – 82.2

8. C – 12

9. A – True

10. D – 47

11. B – False

12. D – 9

13. A – Arizona Cardinals

14. A – Jay Cutler

15. B – 10

16. B – 47.3

17. C – Neck

18. D – Super Bowl MVP

19. A – 44

20. C – Paxton Lynch

DID YOU KNOW?

1. John Elway returned to the club in 2011 as the Broncos President of Football Operations and general manager. He has been a member of the NFL's Competition Committee since 2017 and Elway was the 2015 Executive of the Year after becoming the first person to win a Super Bowl as a starting quarterback and general manager. The Broncos have the seventh-best winning percentage since Elway's return to Denver and, in his 25 years with the program – 16 as a player and nine as an executive – the Broncos have appeared in seven Super Bowls and had just five losing seasons.

2. The Broncos went 21 years between 3,000-yard passers and only had three quarterbacks reach 2,000 yards passing in that intervening two decades. It was part of a rough time for the Broncos quarterbacks after Frank Tripucka's retirement that included just three seasons in which Denver quarterbacks threw more touchdowns than interceptions. The 1960s were a turbulent time for the Broncos after Tripucka left and Denver kept shifting quarterbacks, but things started to settle down in the 1970s with Steve Ramsey and Charley Johnson leading into Craig Morton and, ultimately, John Elway.

3. Marlin Briscoe was drafted by the Broncos to be a cornerback, following in the line of many successful black

college quarterbacks who have been shifted to a different position in the NFL. The only way he would sign with Denver was if the team agreed to a three-day tryout at quarterback, which many believe was rigged against Briscoe from the start. But Denver needed a quarterback that season after an 0-3 start, so the coaches inserted him into the game in the fourth quarter against the Patriots on September 29, 1968. He led the team on an 80-yard touchdown drive, finishing it with a 12-yard scamper, and earned his first start the following week to become the first black quarterback to start a game in modern pro football.

4. Briscoe's name is still firmly entrenched in the Broncos record book for his accomplishments as a rookie. His 14 touchdown passes still stands as the benchmark for Denver's first-year players, along with the 4 touchdowns he threw against Buffalo in November 1968. He was the first Denver rookie to throw for 300 yards in a game and he is also the shortest quarterback ever to suit up for the Broncos.

5. Craig Morton fought through a lot of pain to get the Denver Broncos to their first Super Bowl in franchise history in 1977. Morton had been dealing with a hip injury late in the season and he aggravated it in the divisional round against Pittsburgh. He stayed in the hospital for the entire week leading up to the AFC Championship Game against the Raiders and didn't leave the hospital until the morning of the game. He couldn't

even tie his own shoes before the game – coach Red Miller did the honors – and Miller implored his offensive line to protect the hobbled Morton, who threw 2 touchdown passes to upset the Raiders and lead Denver to the Super Bowl.

6. We almost never saw John Elway the quarterback in the NFL. In his first football game as a sixth-grader in Missoula, Montana, Elway ran for 6 touchdowns in the first half. Thankfully, Jack Elway convinced his son that quarterback was his best position, so we had the legendary No. 7 as a quarterback, not running back. However, Jack couldn't stop John from being elusive on his feet and Elway is the only player in National Football League history to pass for more than 3,000 yards and rush for more than 200 yards in seven consecutive seasons as well as the second to finish his career with 40,000 passing yards and 3,000 rushing yards.

7. The decision was worthwhile in the 1986 AFC Championship Game when Elway completed 6 of 9 passes for 78 yards and scrambled twice for 20 yards as part of the famous "the Drive" to tie the game in the final minute against the Cleveland Browns. Elway then led Denver 60 yards in nine plays in overtime to set up the game-winning field goal, bringing him to his first of five Super Bowl appearances as a player.

8. The Jay Cutler era in Denver was short-lived for a first-round draft pick, but the Broncos certainly sold while the

price was high. His only Pro Bowl season was in 2008, his final of three with Denver, when he threw for 25 touchdowns and a career-high 4,526 yards and was sacked career-low 11 times. He also orchestrated three fourth-quarter comebacks despite the Broncos finishing the season 8-8.

9. Peyton Manning's first three years with the Broncos still hold up as the three best seasons for a Denver quarterback statistically in franchise history. Those three seasons still occupy the top three spots for passing yards and passing touchdowns in a season and three of the top four completion percentage. Few will ever surpass Manning's 2013 season, however, as he still holds the NFL records for passing yards with 5,477 and passing touchdowns with 55 in that campaign.

10. The post-Peyton Manning era has been tough for the Broncos, but they are now pinning their hopes on Drew Lock. The second-year quarterback led Denver to a 4-1 record in the final five games of the 2019 season. Lock completed 64.1 percent of his passes and threw for 1,020 yards and 7 touchdowns while getting picked just three times. Lock became the first rookie in the Super Bowl era to throw for 300 yards and 3 touchdowns in his first road start, a 38-24 win in Houston.

CHAPTER 5:

BETWEEN THE TACKLES

QUIZ TIME!

1. Who led the Broncos in rushing during their inaugural season in 1960?

   a. Al Carmichael

   b. Frank Tripucka

   c. Dave Rolle

   d. Gene Mingo

2. Denver has never had a running back rush the ball 350 times in a single season.

   a. True

   b. False

3. Which of these "delectable" Broncos running backs held the team's single-season rushing record at 954 yards before Floyd Little's arrival in Denver?

   a. Don "The Milkshake" Stone

   b. Charlie "Cake" Mitchell

   c. "Brownie" Billy Joe

   d. Cookie Gilchrist

4. Who was the first Broncos running back to run for 1,000 yards in a season twice?

   a. Otis Armstrong
   b. Floyd Little
   c. Sammy Winder
   d. Bobby Humphrey

5. Gene Mingo accomplished a lot with the Broncos as a member of the first five teams from 1960-64. Which is not one of his accomplishments?

   a. He returned a punt for a touchdown in the first AFL regular-season game Denver played.
   b. He was the first African-American placekicker in professional football.
   c. He threw for a touchdown, ran for a touchdown, and caught a touchdown pass in his career.
   d. He led pro football in scoring through his first four seasons in the league.

6. In which year did Floyd Little lead the NFL in rushing with 1,133 yards?

   a. 1970
   b. 1971
   c. 1972
   d. 1973

7. Floyd Little still holds the record for most all-purpose yards with the Denver Broncos.

   a. True
   b. False

8. How many consecutive times did Floyd Little lead the Broncos in rushing, a mark that still stands as the franchise record?

    a. 4
    b. 5
    c. 6
    d. 7

9. In which two seasons did Bobby Humphrey become the first Denver running back to run for 1,000 yards in consecutive years?

    a. 1987 & 1988
    b. 1988 & 1989
    c. 1989 & 1990
    d. 1990 & 1991

10. From 1995 until 2006, at least one Broncos player ran for at least 1,000 yards each season.

    a. True
    b. False

11. Terrell Davis set the franchise record for most rushing yards in a season in 1998 when he ran for how many yards, a total that ranks fourth in NFL history?

    a. 1,997
    b. 2,001
    c. 2,008
    d. 2,016

12. How many touchdowns did Terrell Davis rush for in his Broncos career?

    a. 60
    b. 65
    c. 70
    d. 75

13. Which of these Denver running backs had multiple 1,000-yard rushing seasons for the Broncos?

    a. Knowshon Moreno
    b. Mike Anderson
    c. Tatum Bell
    d. Willis McGahee

14. Against which team did Mike Anderson set the Broncos' single-game rushing record?

    a. Oakland Raiders
    b. Dallas Cowboys
    c. New Orleans Saints
    d. Green Bay Packers

15. Who was the running back Denver selected with the draft pick it received in the Clinton Portis trade with Washington?

    a. Shaun Draughn
    b. Maurice Clarett
    c. Quentin Griffin
    d. Tatum Bell

16. How many yards did Denver rush for against Chicago in the 1976 season finale while setting the franchise record for most team rushing yards in a game?

a. 356

b. 364

c. 377

d. 389

17. How much was the signing bonus Phillip Lindsay received when he inked with the Broncos as an undrafted free agent in 2018?

a. $10,000

b. $15,000

c. $20,000

d. $25,000

18. Denver drafted all of its top eight rushers in career yards.

a. True

b. False

19. How many rushing touchdowns did Clinton Portis have when he set the franchise record against Kansas City in 2003?

a. 3

b. 4

c. 5

d. 6

20. Who was the last running back to lead Denver in rushing yards without leading the team in rushing attempts?

a. C.J. Anderson

b. Peyton Hillis

c. Phillip Lindsay

d. Travis Henry

QUIZ ANSWERS

1. C – Dave Rolle

2. B – False

3. D – Cookie Gilchrist

4. A – Otis Armstrong

5. D – He led pro football in scoring through his first four seasons in the league.

6. B – 1970

7. B – False

8. D – 7

9. C – 1989 & 1990

10. B – False

11. C – 2,008

12. A – 60

13. B – Mike Anderson

14. C – New Orleans Saints

15. D – Tatum Bell

16. A – 356

17. B – $15,000

18. A – True

19. C – 5

20. B – Peyton Hillis

DID YOU KNOW?

1. Floyd Little was the first Broncos first-round pick who actually signed with Denver, which coincided with the first combined draft between the AFL and NFL. From 1967-1975, only O.J. Simpson ran for more yards than Little across professional football, and Little now ranks second behind Terrell Davis in every major statistical category in Broncos history. He played in five All-Star games in six years as a member of the AFL All-Star Game in 1968 and 69 then being voted into the Pro Bowl in 1970, 1971, and 1973. He was finally elected into the Hall of Fame in 2010 after being nominated by the Veterans Committee.

2. Billy Joe led the Broncos in rushing in 1963 and then became part of the trade that brought Cookie Gilchrist to Denver for one season. However, his greatest impact came as a college coach. He led Central State in Ohio to the 1983 NCAA Division II national championship game and then led them to NAIA national titles in 1990 and 1992 after the school made the transition for the 1987 season. He left for Florida A&M in 1994, winning a conference title in 1995 and helping the Rattlers qualify for the Division I-AA playoffs six straight seasons, including a 1999 run to the national semifinals. He ranks second to Eddie Robinson in on the all-time black college coaching wins list.

3. Almost a third of Otis Armstrong's rushing yards in eight seasons with the Broncos came in his second season with the team in 1974. Armstrong ran for 1,407 yards in a season marred by a strike by the players during training camp. He ran for a then-record 183 yards in the season finale to secure consecutive winning seasons for the team. He responded to a tough 1975 season with another 1,000-yard campaign in 1976, but he never ran for more than 500 yards in any of his last four seasons in Denver.

4. Sammy Winder is the most unheralded of the feature backs that played for the Broncos in the team's history. He's the only other running back besides Terrell Davis and Floyd Little to lead Denver in rushing in three consecutive seasons, doing so five straight seasons from 1983 to 1987. He had only one 1,000-yard year – 1,153 yards in 1984 – but he played a key role in Denver's success in John Elway's early years as a player. He ranks third all-time in rushing yards with 5,427 over nine seasons with the franchise and he had just eight 100-yard games with the franchise.

5. Terrell Davis was basically unstoppable in the 1997 and 1998 postseasons, which ended with the Broncos consecutive Super Bowl victories. He ran for at least 100 yards in all seven games Denver played in those two seasons, an NFL record for consecutive 100-yard rushing games in the playoffs, finishing with 1,049 yards across those two playoffs runs. He scored 8 touchdowns in four games while leading Denver to its first Super Bowl title in

the 1997 season, capping it off with Super Bowl MVP honors against the Packers. The following season, he set the Broncos' postseason record with 199 yards against Miami in the divisional round.

6. Davis' performance in the 1998 season was one of the best ever for a running back in NFL history. He became the fourth player to ever rush for 2,000 yards in a season and ran for 100 or more yards in a team record 11 of Denver's 16 games that season, including a team record seven straight games. During that stretch, he ran for 100 yards in a quarter three times and had his third and final career 200-yard game with 208 yards against Seattle. He was the NFL MVP that season and ran for 21 touchdowns, which stands as Denver's single-season record and it was the third of three consecutive First Team All-Pro seasons.

7. Mike Anderson had an explosive rookie year for Denver in 2000, taking the league by storm as a sixth-round pick out of Utah. He started 12 games for the Broncos that season and ran for 1,487 yards and 15 touchdowns. He is the only rookie ever to rush for 175 yards in three different games, one of which was his franchise-record 251 yards against the New Orleans Saints on December 3. Injuries limited him over the next four seasons, but he returned in 2005 to rush for 1,000 yards again for Denver, earning him a contract with Baltimore. He still ranks fifth in Denver history in rushing yards and fourth in touchdowns.

8. Clinton Portis wasn't a member of the Broncos for long, but his two seasons in Denver still make him one of the best to ever play for the franchise. He played in just 29 games, but he ranks eighth on the Broncos' rushing list with 3,099 yards. His 1,508 yards as a rookie still stands as the team record for first-year players and the 5.5 yards per carry he averaged in his two seasons with the team is a franchise record as well. His 29 touchdowns is sixth-most in franchise history and his five-touchdown performance, the one he told ESPN was the reason he was traded after the 2003 season, is still the Denver record.

9. Mike Shanahan's final season as Broncos head coach in 2008 produced a very odd year rushing. Peyton Hillis' 343 yards were the fewest to lead Denver in rushing in the team's history, but four different running backs started games for the Broncos that season. Three of those four running backs averaged at least five yards per carry and Denver still finished in the middle of the league in rushing yards. Sparked by the instability at running back, the Broncos drafted Knowshon Moreno with its 2009 first-round pick.

10. The Phillip Lindsay story has many twists and turns, many of which fans already know. Lindsay tore his ACL in his senior year of high school the same night he broke his dad's career rushing record in the Denver Public School District. Most of his Division I offers were pulled, but Colorado stuck by him and then Lindsay went surprisingly undrafted in 2018 after being a surprise

omission from the NFL Combine. In an interview with Peter King, he told the veteran journalist that his mother told him to stay home and play for the Broncos, and that is why he ended up signing with Denver.

CHAPTER 6:

CATCHING THE BALL

QUIZ TIME!

1. Lionel Taylor did not surpass 1,000 yards receiving in Denver's first season in 1960.

   a. True
   b. False

2. Who caught the longest touchdown pass in Bronco history?

   a. Rod Smith
   b. Shannon Sharpe
   c. Jerry Tarr
   d. Steve Watson

3. Who holds the team record for most consecutive games with a touchdown reception with 7?

   a. Haven Moses
   b. Riley Odoms
   c. Vance Johnson
   d. Wes Welker

4. Whose average reception gain of 20.5 yards is the most in Broncos history?

   a. Bill Van Heusen
   b. Ashley Lelie
   c. Al Frazier
   d. Haven Moses

5. Which wide receiver holds the record for the longest pass thrown by a rookie in Broncos history?

   a. Arthur Marshall
   b. Rod Smith
   c. Eddie Royal
   d. Brandon Marshall

6. Who shares the record with Demaryius Thomas with 14 touchdown catches in a season?

   a. Brandon Marshall
   b. Julius Thomas
   c. Rod Smith
   d. Anthony Miller

7. What was the most passes Lionel Taylor ever caught in a game for the Broncos?

   a. 10
   b. 12
   c. 13
   d. 15

8. Lionel Taylor had 100 receptions in his second year with the Broncos in 1961. When was the next time a Denver receiver had at least 100 catches in a season?

a. 1979

b. 1986

c. 1994

d. 2000

9. What was the fewest number of receptions Lionel Taylor had in his first six seasons with the Broncos?

a. 72

b. 76

c. 81

d. 84

10. Shannon Sharpe did not catch a touchdown pass in either of Denver's postseason runs to the Super Bowl.

a. True

b. False

11. Shannon Sharpe led Denver in receptions five times, but how many times did he lead the Broncos in receiving yards?

a. 1

b. 2

c. 3

d. 4

12. Shannon Sharpe played 12 of his 14 NFL seasons with the Broncos. Where did he sign for 2000 and 2001, when he ultimately broke the NFL records for receptions and receiving yards for a tight end?

a. Miami Dolphins

b. Green Bay Packers

c. San Francisco 49ers

d. Baltimore Ravens

13. In how many consecutive games did Rod Smith catch a pass, setting a franchise record?

    a. 112

    b. 116

    c. 120

    d. 124

14. Rod Smith holds all three of the Broncos' major career receiving records, but which is the only single-season record he still holds?

    a. Touchdown receptions

    b. Receiving yards

    c. Receptions

    d. Average gain per reception

15. In how many seasons did Brandon Marshall lead the Broncos in receptions, receiving yards, and receiving touchdowns?

    a. 2

    b. 3

    c. 1

    d. 4

16. Against whom did Brandon Marshall set the NFL record with 21 receptions in 2009?

    a. Indianapolis Colts

    b. New England Patriots

c. Kansas City Chiefs

d. Buffalo Bills

17. Eddie Royal is the only Denver Broncos wide receiver to eclipse 1,000 yards receiving as a rookie

a. True

b. False

18. How many touchdown passes did Demaryius Thomas haul in when he broke the franchise's single-season receiving yards record in 2014?

a. 14

b. 13

c. 12

d. 11

19. Who is the only Broncos player to catch 4 touchdown passes in a single game?

a. Demaryius Thomas

b. Shannon Sharpe

c. Rod Smith

d. Eric Decker

20. Which of these receivers never had a 1,000-yard season for the Broncos?

a. Javon Walker

b. Ashley Lelie

c. Mark Jackson

d. Ed McCaffrey.

QUIZ ANSWERS

1. B – False

2. C – Jerry Tarr

3. B – Riley Odoms

4. A – Bill Van Heusen

5. A – Arthur Marshall

6. D – Anthony Miller

7. C – 13

8. D – 2000

9. B – 76

10. A – True

11. B – 2

12. D – Baltimore Ravens

13. D – 124

14. C – Receptions

15. B – 3

16. A – Indianapolis Colts

17. B – False

18. D – 11

19. D – Eric Decker

20. C – Mark Jackson

DID YOU KNOW?

1. Lionel Taylor played one season with the Chicago Bears in the NFL before joining the Broncos for their inaugural season. However, Taylor was drafted as a linebacker for the Bears, but he didn't even last the full season at linebacker before switching to defensive back. He told the Broncos official website, "I never liked to tackle anybody, which is why I switched from linebacker to defensive back for the Chicago Bears and then eventually became a receiver. But you could hit me all day long. I really didn't mind." After being cut by the Bears, Taylor played semi-professional football in California, which is how he was discovered by Denver general manager Dean Griffing, who signed him to the Broncos.

2. Rick Upchurch is the only Broncos player to ever appear on two different All-Decade teams as voted upon by the Pro Football Hall of Fame Selection Committee. Upchurch was not known for his receiving abilities as much as his explosiveness as a kick and punt returner. He caught just 267 passes in nine seasons with the team, but he scored 8 touchdowns on 248 punt returns, which was the NFL record when he retired and is still the Broncos team record. In 1976, his second year in the league, he tied the NFL record with 4 punt-return touchdowns, a mark that still hasn't been broken.

3. Haven Moses averaged at least 19 yards per catch in three consecutive seasons from 1976-78 with the Broncos. The following year, he had the best season of his career with 54 catches for 943 yards to help Denver return to the playoffs for a third straight year. In 1977, Moses caught 2 touchdown passes in the AFC Championship Game to help the Broncos reach the Super Bowl for the first time in franchise history. He caught one pass for 21 yards in that loss to Dallas in Super Bowl XII.

4. For five years, from 1981 through 1985, Steve Watson was the go-to receiver for the Broncos. He had a breakthrough season in 1981, his third season with Denver since signing as an undrafted free agent out of Temple. That season, Watson caught 60 passes for a career-best 1,244 yards and 13 touchdowns. He had two more 1,000-yard seasons, in 1983 and 1984, with John Elway helming the offense and then came 85 yards short of 1,000 yards in 1985.

5. In his Hall of Fame induction speech, Shannon Sharpe shared a story of how close he came to not being the greatest tight end ever to play for the Broncos. In the final preseason game of his rookie year, he said he was told by a coach that his name was on the board to be cut before the start of the season. Sharpe said he knew he had to put something on tape so other teams would know he could play and potentially sign him. In the pouring rain, Sharpe played 20 offensive plays and on special teams and registered 12 knockdown blocks. The next day, the Broncos coaches took his name off the cut board.

6. Rod Smith made an immediate impact in Denver from the first time he stepped onto the field in a Broncos uniform. His first career catch on September 17, 1995, was a last-second game-winning 43-yard touchdown strike from John Elway to lift Denver over Washington. He was only a three-time Pro Bowl selection but he retired in 2007 holding every major career receiving record for the Broncos. His 11,389 career receiving yards ranks second to Antonio Gates among undrafted players in league history.

7. Ed McCaffrey was largely overshadowed by Shannon Sharpe and Rod Smith during his nine years in Denver, from 1995 through 2003. He had three 1,000-yard seasons for the team but he never led the team in receiving yards. He had 101 catches in 2000, the only time he led the team in that statistic, but he led the Broncos in touchdown receptions three straight years, 1998-2000. He ranks fifth in franchise history in receptions and receiving yards and he is fourth with 46 touchdown catches.

8. Brandon Marshall was extremely productive in his four seasons with the Broncos. After being selected in the fourth round of the 2006 NFL draft, Marshall had three straight 1,000-yard seasons, from 2007 through 1909, before he was traded to Miami. The trade winds started swirling in 2009 when Marshall was suspended during training camp for an outburst based on his frustration over not having a new contract and the team's medical staff misdiagnosing a hip injury. Although he might have been disgruntled, Marshall still is the only Broncos player

with three 100-catch seasons and ranks 10th in Broncos history for career receptions.

9. The Broncos fortunes of drafting receivers continued in 2010 with first-round pick Demaryius Thomas. The Georgia Tech product surpassed Shannon Sharpe for second on the Broncos career list for receiving yards and touchdowns during his nine seasons in Denver. Thomas holds three of the top four receiving-yard seasons in team history as well as the team record for single-game receiving yards. He had five 1,000-yard seasons and a team record 36 games with at least 100 yards receiving, 10 of which came in 2014, when he had a franchise-best seven straight games with at least 100 yards while setting the record for most receiving yards in a season.

10. The Broncos won the AFC West in 2011 with arguably the worst passing offense in the league. Eric Decker's 612 yards were the fewest to lead the Broncos in almost 30 seasons and his 44 catches were the fewest since 1987 to lead Denver. Only two receivers had at least 20 catches that season – Decker and Demaryius Thomas – and the same duo were the only ones to surpass 300 receiving yards. That pair also caught 12 of the team's 20 touchdown passes in the regular season

CHAPTER 7:

TRENCH WARFARE

QUIZ TIME!

1. Which pass rusher is among those tied for an NFL record with 10 straight games with a sack?

    a. Simon Fletcher

    b. Von Miller

    c. Karl Mecklenburg

    d. Elvis Dumervil

2. Which pass rusher has not had at least 20 games with multiple sacks for the Broncos?

    a. Elvis Dumervil

    b. Simon Fletcher

    c. Barney Chavous

    d. Von Miller

3. How many times has a Broncos player tied the franchise record with 4 sacks in a game?

    a. 5

    b. 6

c. 7

d. 8

4. Who is the only Broncos player to have multiple career safeties for the franchise?

   a. Tom Jackson

   b. Simon Fletcher

   c. Elvis Dumervil

   d. Rulon Jones

5. What is the Broncos record for most sacks in a game since the sack became an official NFL stat in 1982?

   a. 10

   b. 9

   c. 8

   d. 7

6. Which of these offensive linemen did not start both of Denver's Super Bowl victories in 1997 and 1998?

   a. Mark Schlereth

   b. Gary Zimmerman

   c. Tony Jones

   d. Tom Nalen

7. Which offensive lineman is tied with Jason Elam as the second longest-tenured Broncos player with 15 seasons with the team?

   a. Mark Schlereth

   b. Paul Howard

   c. Ken Lanier

   d. Tom Nalen

8. Louis Vasquez was the last Broncos offensive lineman to be named to an All-Pro team.

    a. True
    b. False

9. Which guard took over at center in 2002, when Tom Nalen missed time with a torn ligament in his left knee?

    a. Ben Hamilton
    b. Dan Neil
    c. Steve Herndon
    d. Lennie Friedman

10. How many members of the 2019 starting offensive line did the Broncos draft?

    a. 1
    b. 2
    c. 3
    d. 4

11. How many consecutive games did Simon Fletcher play with the Broncos to set the team record for consecutive appearances?

    a. 172
    b. 175
    c. 184
    d. 187

12. How many career postseason sacks does Simon Fletcher own in 12 playoff games?

    a. 6
    b. 7

c. 9.5

d. 11

13. Randy Gradishar has been a semifinalist for the Pro Football Hall of Fame four times, but he's never been a finalist for induction.

a. True

b. False

14. Karl Mecklenburg had six seasons with at least 100 tackles and in 1989 he had his career high with how many stops?

a. 126

b. 132

c. 139

d. 143

15. Which team originally drafted Hall-of-Famer Gary Zimmerman in 1984?

a. Denver Broncos

b. Los Angeles Rams

c. Minnesota Vikings

d. New York Giants

16. Which defensive lineman was the first to play 10 seasons for the Broncos?

a. Barney Chavous

b. Rich Jackson

c. Paul Smith

d. Lyle Alzado

17. Who is the only player to be named the Associated Press NFL Defensive Player of the Year?

    a. Karl Mecklenburg
    b. Von Miller
    c. Simon Fletcher
    d. Randy Gradishar

18. Who was the first Broncos player to return a blocked field goal for a touchdown?

    a. Simon Fletcher
    b. John Bramlett
    c. Rich Jackson
    d. Jerry Hopkins

19. In which season did Denver set its record for fewest sacks allowed with only 12?

    a. 1998
    b. 2004
    c. 2008
    d. 2015

20. Von Miller's rookie season was the only time he was not named an All-Pro in his first eight seasons in the league.

    a. True
    b. False

QUIZ ANSWERS

1. A – Simon Fletcher

2. C – Barney Chavous

3. C – 7

4. D – Rulon Jones

5. B – 9

6. B – Gary Zimmerman

7. D – Tom Nalen

8. A – True

9. A – Ben Hamilton

10. C – 3

11. A – 172

12. A – 6

13. B – False

14. D – 143

15. D – New York Giants

16. C – Paul Smith

17. D – Randy Gradishar

18. B – John Bramlett

19. C – 2008

20. B – False

DID YOU KNOW?

1. It took some bad luck for the Broncos to end up acquiring Gary Zimmerman from Minnesota. In the first year of full-fledged free agency in 1993, Denver signed Don Maggs, who had been protecting Warren Moon in Houston for years. Maggs suffered an injury during that offseason and the Broncos knew they needed to find a left tackle for John Elway. They reached out to Minnesota, which was in a contract dispute with Zimmerman at the time and agreed to trade the future Hall-of-Famer to Denver right before the season began. Zimmerman went on to anchor the Denver offensive line for the next five seasons before retiring after Super Bowl XXXII.

2. Most people probably now remember Tom Jackson as an NFL analyst for ESPN rather than his prolific career with the Broncos. Jackson played his entire 14-year career with Denver and was named the team's defensive MVP three times by his teammates. He was a three-time Pro Bowler and two-time First Team All-Pro linebacker, who holds the team record for most interceptions by a linebacker with 20. He had a career-best 169 tackles in 1980 as part of 11 straight years as one of the team's top five tacklers. In 2015, he was awarded the Pete Rozelle Radio-Television Award by the Pro Football Hall of Fame for his more than 30 years on analysis with ESPN.

3. Stan Jones was enshrined in the Pro Football Hall of Fame as a player for the Chicago Bears, but he spent 18 years as an assistant coach in Denver before his 1991 induction. Jones was the defensive line coach for Denver's first three Super Bowl appearances and was a key defensive coach for the Orange Crush defense. He was a Broncos assistant from 1967 through 1971 under Lou Saban and then joined Saban in Buffalo from 1972 through 1976. He rejoined the Denver staff for John Ralston's final season as head coach, then stuck around for Red Miller's tenure and most of Dan Reeves' success in Denver before retiring after the 1988 season.

4. In 1960, the AFL released its draft results, with each team's picks listed in alphabetical order. However, the Broncos count Trinity College center Roger LeClerc as the team's first-ever draft pick. Over the next six seasons, Denver drafted an offensive tackle with its first pick three times, including drafting future Hall-of-Famer Merlin Olsen in 1962.

5. Simon Fletcher went from smoking offensive linemen and quarterbacks to smoking meats in his post-NFL life. Fletcher retired as the Broncos' all-time leader in sacks with 97.5 after playing in 172 consecutive games for the franchise and he still owns three of the six best single-season sack totals. Since retiring, he has opened two barbecue restaurants in Colorado. He opened his first joint, Whistle Blowers Grill & BBQ, in Greeley in 2013, but it was closed in 2016 due to the building being condemned. He

came back with Simon Fletcher's Gridiron Grill and BBQ a few months later in 2016 and it's still in operation.

6. Randy Gradishar has strong backing for induction into the Pro Football Hall of Fame but he has yet to earn that famous knock on the day before the Super Bowl. In 2003 and 2008, Gradishar was a finalist and even made it to the final 10 in 2003 but, between those two appearances as a finalist, he was cut during the semifinal round each time. He was a finalist for the Centennial Class in 2020, but again didn't make the cut. He was the consensus Defensive Player of the Year in 1978 when he had a team record 286 tackles and he was a seven-time Pro Bowler, as well.

7. Karl Mecklenburg is the only Broncos player to have 4 sacks in a game twice, and both of those came in the 1985 season. He had 13 sacks that season, which stood as the Broncos' record for a year before it was broken by Rulon Jones. Mecklenburg played 12 seasons for the Broncos, suffered a dozen or so concussions, and was named as a plaintiff in the major lawsuit brought against the NFL in 2012. In one 2019 talk, he told the audience, "I didn't buy into professional football with the understanding that I was going to have brain damage. I expected to have a limp. I expected to have sore joints. Bad shoulder, whatever. But that other part, that was kept from us and that wasn't right."

8. It is hard to judge a center's worthiness for the Pro Football Hall of Fame, but three-time All-Pro center Tom

Nalen would certainly fit the bill. Nalen is one of several Broncos that fans and Denver media have advocated for inclusion in Canton. The Broncos won 62.5 percent of their games in the 13 seasons Nalen was the starting center and six different running backs had a total of 11 1,000-yard rushing season. Denver finished in the top 10 in rushing offenses 12 times in those 13 years, including nine seasons in the top five.

9. The Broncos thought they had drafted the next cornerstone of its offensive line in 2008 when they selected Boise State tackle Ryan Clady in the first round. After allowing just half a sack as a rookie, Clady was a four-time Pro Bowl selection and two-time All-Pro honoree. However, he suffered a Lisfranc injury early in the 2013 season that sidelined him for 14 games, and then he missed the 2015 Super Bowl run with a torn ACL. He signed with the New York Jets for the 2016 season but missed almost half of that season with a shoulder injury before retiring in 2017.

10. No one has rushed the quarterback for the Denver Broncos better than Von Miller, the team's selection with the second overall pick in the 2011 NFL draft. Miller holds the team's career sacks record with 106 in his first nine seasons in the league and he broke the single-season mark with 18.5 in 2012. He is the only player with more than 2 sacks in a playoff game, and he did it twice in Denver's run to the Super Bowl in 2015. He has 24 games with multiple sacks and went nine straight games with a sack in 2018.

CHAPTER 8:

NO AIR ZONE

QUIZ TIME!

1. Who holds the record for most career interceptions for Denver?

    a. Champ Bailey

    b. Austin "Goose" Gonsoulin

    c. Steve Foley

    d. Louis Wright

2. Which of these Hall of Fame defensive backs never played with the Broncos?

    a. Brian Dawkins

    b. Rod Woodson

    c. Ty Law

    d. Willie Brown

3. Austin "Goose" Gonsoulin holds the record for most interceptions in a season with 12.

    a. True

    b. False

4. Which of these players does not own a share of the Broncos record of 4 interceptions in one game?

   a. Champ Bailey
   b. Deltha O'Neal
   c. Willie Brown
   d. Austin "Goose" Gonsoulin

5. When did Champ Bailey set the Broncos record with interceptions in 5 consecutive games?

   a. 2008
   b. 2007
   c. 2006
   d. 2005

6. What is the record for the lowest completion percentage allowed by the Broncos in a season?

   a. 42.1
   b. 43.4
   c. 44.6
   d. 45.2

7. When was the last time Denver had 5 interceptions in a game?

   a. 2013
   b. 2007
   c. 2005
   d. 2001

8. How many times have the Broncos returned an interception for a touchdown?

a. 84

b. 89

c. 93

d. 96

9. Aqib Talib returned more than half of his interceptions with the Broncos for touchdowns and still has the record for most career pick-sixes with 6.

a. True

b. False

10. In 2018, the Broncos returned two interceptions for a touchdown in the same game for the fourth time in their franchise history. Who was Denver playing when it accomplished that feat?

a. Seattle Seahawks

b. Arizona Cardinals

c. Los Angeles Rams

d. New England Patriots

11. The 1976 Broncos hold the team record for fewest passing touchdowns allowed. How many did Denver allow that season?

a. 10

b. 7

c. 9

d. 8

12. Which College Football Hall of Fame coach gave Austin Gonsoulin his nickname of Goose?

a. Woody Hayes

b. Bear Bryant

c. Joe Paterno

d. Hayden Fry

13. Austin "Goose" Gonsoulin was one of the first four Broncos elected to the team's Ring of Fame in 1984.

a. True

b. False

14. Billy Thompson holds the record for most consecutive starts for Denver. How many straight games did he start for the Broncos?

a. 149

b. 153

c. 156

d. 162

15. Which word did Steve Atwater use in this quote about his style of play: "I've always tried to be _____. I don't always make all the tackles or make all the big hits, but I try to play in a(n) _____ manner."

a. Intelligent

b. Aggressive

c. Physical

d. Unpredictable

16. How many passes did Steve Atwater intercept during his 10 seasons in Denver?

a. 21

b. 24

c. 26

d. 29

17. Champ Bailey owns the record for the longest non-scoring play in NFL history.

    a. True

    b. False

18. Champ Bailey has the most Pro Bowl honors of any defensive back in NFL history. How many times was he selected for the Pro Bowl?

    a. 9

    b. 10

    c. 11

    d. 12

19. Who was the last player to intercept at least 5 passes in a season for the Broncos?

    a. Aqib Talib

    b. Justin Simmons

    c. Andre Goodman

    d. Chris Harris Jr.

20. Bradley Roby is the last defensive back the Broncos drafted in the first round. What was his highest interception total in his five seasons in Denver?

    a. 1

    b. 2

    c. 3

    d. 4

QUIZ ANSWERS

1. C – Steve Foley

2. B – Rod Woodson

3. B – False

4. A – Champ Bailey

5. D – 2005

6. A – 42.1

7. D – 2001

8. C – 93

9. A – True

10. B – Arizona Cardinals

11. D – 8

12. D – Hayden Fry

13. A – True

14. C – 156

15. B – Aggressive

16. B – 24

17. A – True

18. D – 12

19. C – Andre Goodman

20. B – 2

DID YOU KNOW?

1. Billy Thompson could do it all for the Broncos, which is a main reason why he leads the franchise in career takeaways with 61 over a 13-year career in Denver. He held the NFL record for most fumbles returned for touchdowns for many years and he is Denver's career leader with 784 interception return yards. Yet he also made big contributions on special teams for the Broncos. As a rookie, Thompson led the league in both kickoff returns and punt returns in 1969, the first player in professional football to lead a league in both categories.

2. Willie Brown had a far different interpretation of his position than most people who watch defensive backs in current times. He was once quoted as saying, "My job was not catching passes. My job was to stop the receiver from catching it. If I could have played 15 or 20 years without an interception, that would have been fine. Anything beyond stopping a receiver, that's gravy." Yet Brown was pretty good at intercepting passes as a method to prevent receivers from catching the ball. Brown signed with the Broncos in 1963 after being cut by the Houston Oilers as an undrafted free agent and had 9 interceptions as a second-year pro, including his record-tying 4 against the New York Jets.

3. Steve Atwater's Hall of Fame career with Denver was bookended by Super Bowl appearances. He made 129

tackles as a rookie to help the Broncos defense lead Denver to the Super Bowl in the 1989 season, and then helped the Broncos win Super Bowls in 1997 and 1998. He holds the franchise record with seven consecutive Pro Bowl appearances from 1990-1996 and added an eighth honor in 1998, his final season with the team.

4. Before Steve Foley became Denver's all-time leader in interceptions, he tried his hand as a quarterback in the World Football League. He played one season for the Jacksonville Express in 1975 after being drafted in the eighth round by the Broncos but quickly discovered he had a better chance as a defensive back. As a vital member of the Orange Crush defense during his 11 seasons in Denver, Foley led the Broncos in interceptions outright three times and tied for the lead on two other occasions. If not for a broken forearm that sidelined him after the first game of the 1982 season, Foley likely would have been further ahead in the record books and in the team's Ring of Fame.

5. The man trailing Foley by one in career interceptions holds two records no one will ever reach. Austin "Goose" Gonsoulin earned his nickname returning punts at Baylor, but he will forever be known as the AFL's interception king. His 43 career interceptions were the most by anyone in the AFL's brief existence and he also happened to have the AFL's first interception as well. He's the only Broncos player with at least 3 interceptions in two different games, becoming the first Denver player with 4 in a game as a

rookie against Buffalo in 1960. He intercepted Kansas City's Len Dawson three times in 1964 and, at halftime of that game, Dawson actually came over and cursed him out because he was so mad.

6. Champ Bailey was the other end of the famous 2004 trade between Denver and Washington and both franchises will argue about who got the better end of the deal. The trade talks began at the Senior Bowl that season when Bailey's agent, who also represented Broncos kicker Jason Elam, told Denver's management about Washington's decision to apply the franchise tag to Bailey. At the Super Bowl that season, Denver's top brass were in the same suite as Washington owner Dan Snyder and the trade was discussed further. Once the terms were settled, Bailey still had to sign his franchise tag to make the deal official and he said he wouldn't have signed the contract if he didn't like the trade.

7. Louis Wright's path to NFL stardom was a long one from Bakersfield High School to the Broncos. Wright began at Arizona State on a football scholarship but then transferred to Bakersfield College in order to both play football and run track. He estimates that he played just six or seven snaps the entire season, so he quit the football team to focus on track and field. That was the sport that earned him a spot at San Jose State and he figured his football career was done. But San Jose State hired a new football coach the year Wright arrived and the new staff went to watch track practice to look for some speed.

Wright's speed and previous football experience made him the perfect fit and he made his debut for the Spartans against Arizona State.

8. Aqib Talib was a wizard with the ball in his hands after intercepting passes. He only picked off 11 throws in his four years with Denver, but he holds the franchise record with an average return of 34 yards. The cornerback returned a team-high 6 of his 11 interceptions for touchdowns, including a 103-yard score in 2017 against Dallas that also is a Denver record. In all, 318 of his 374 return yards came on his 5 scores, which still leaves him with a respectable 11.2-yard average for his non-scoring interceptions.

9. Before Champ Bailey joined the Broncos, his No. 24 was worn by 2000 first-round pick Deltha O'Neal, who had an interesting career in Denver. O'Neal didn't have an interception as a rookie and was only credited with three passes defended, but was a returner for the Broncos. He exploded in 2001 with 9 interceptions and 25 passes defended and then had 5 picks the following year while starting 30 of the 32 games those two seasons. In 2003, he made a brief appearance as a wide receiver due to his speed but made just two catches on three targets in the failed experiment to go along with just one interception on defense. He was traded to Cincinnati in 2004 then had a career year in 2005 before flaming out again.

10. The 2019 season was the first time since 2010 that the Broncos didn't have an interception returned for a

touchdown. It's only happened 17 times in the Broncos' history with the longest streak of consecutive seasons with a pick-six being the 11 years from 1995-2007.

CHAPTER 9:

SUPER BOWL SALUTE

QUIZ TIME!

1. How many times has Denver played in the Super Bowl?

    a. 6

    b. 7

    c. 8

    d. 9

2. Who did the Broncos play in the only Super Bowl in which they scored two touchdowns and still lost?

    a. San Francisco 49ers

    b. Seattle Seahawks

    c. Washington Redskins

    d. New York Giants

3. Which of these players was never a Super Bowl MVP for the Broncos?

    a. Peyton Manning

    b. John Elway

    c. Von Miller

    d. Terrell Davis

4. In which city has Denver not won a Super Bowl?

    a. Santa Clara

    b. New Orleans

    c. San Diego

    d. Miami

5. Who scored the first points for Denver in Super Bowl XII?

    a. Otis Armstrong

    b. Jim Turner

    c. Rob Lytle

    d. Craig Morton

6. Craig Morton completed as many passes to his teammates as he did the Cowboys in Super Bowl XII.

    a. True

    b. False

7. Which play gave the Broncos their first-ever lead in a Super Bowl against the Giants in Super Bowl XXI?

    a. A Sammy Winder touchdown run

    b. A John Elway touchdown pass

    c. A Rich Karlis field goal

    d. A John Elway touchdown run

8. Who was on the receiving end of John Elway's fourth-quarter touchdown pass that was Denver's first passing touchdown in a Super Bowl?

    a. Riley Odoms

    b. Sammy Winder

    c. Gerald Willhite

    d. Vance Johnson

9. Denver has the record for most points allowed in the second half of a Super Bowl after allowing 30 points to the Giants in Super Bowl XXI. The following year, the Broncos set the record for points allowed in the first half and in any quarter, when they allowed Washington to score how many points in the second quarter of Super Bowl XXII?

    a. 28
    b. 31
    c. 35
    d. 42

10. The Broncos became the first team to ever lose consecutive Super Bowls after falling to Washington in Super Bowl XXII.

    a. True
    b. False

11. John Elway caught only one pass in a postseason game, and it came in Super Bowl XXII against Washington. Who threw that 23-yard pass to Elway?

    a. Sammy Winder
    b. Gene Lang
    c. Steve Sewell
    d. Ricky Nattiel

12. Who scored Denver's only touchdown in the biggest blowout in Super Bowl history against San Francisco in Super Bowl XXIV?

a. Steve Atwater

b. Steve Sewell

c. Bobby Humphrey

d. John Elway

13. The Broncos did not score a touchdown of more than one yard in their Super Bowl XXXII win over Green Bay.

a. True

b. False

14. How long was Jason Elam's field goal in Super Bowl XXXII against the Packers that is the longest in Denver's Super Bowl history?

a. 51 yards

b. 50 yards

c. 49 yards

d. 52 yards

15. Why did Terrell Davis basically miss a quarter of Super Bowl XXXII?

a. Broken finger

b. Ankle sprain

c. Hamstring strain

d. Migraines

16. Who scored multiple touchdowns in Denver's rout of Atlanta in Super Bowl XXXIII?

a. John Elway

b. Rod Smith

c. Howard Griffith

d. Terrell Davis

17. How many passing yards did John Elway have in Super Bowl XXXIII in his MVP-winning effort?

    a. 324
    b. 336
    c. 352
    d. 365

18. Who fell on the Cam Newton fumble that Von Miller forced in the first quarter of Super Bowl 50?

    a. Chris Harris Jr.
    b. Malik Jackson
    c. DeMarcus Ware
    d. Von Miller

19. John Elway and Gary Kubiak teamed up to help the Broncos win Super Bowl 50 as general manager and coach, respectively. How many times did the two of them lose the Super Bowl together as quarterbacks with Denver?

    a. 3
    b. 1
    c. 4
    d. 2

20. Denver set its franchise record for most sacks in a playoff game in its win over Carolina in Super Bowl 50. How many sacks did the Broncos record to take home their third Super Bowl title?

    a. 5
    b. 6
    c. 7
    d. 8

QUIZ ANSWERS

1. C – 8

2. D – New York Giants

3. A – Peyton Manning

4. B – New Orleans

5. B – Jim Turner

6. A – True

7. C – A Rich Karlis field goal

8. D – Vance Johnson

9. C – 35

10. B – False

11. C – Steve Sewell

12. D – John Elway

13. A – True

14. A – 51 yards

15. D – Migraines

16. C – Howard Griffith

17. B – 336

18. B – Malik Jackson

19. A – 3

20. C – 7

DID YOU KNOW?

1. The Broncos have been on the wrong end of some of the worst losses in Super Bowl history, including the most lopsided championship game in the Super Bowl era. In three of Denver's five Super Bowl losses, the Broncos have allowed at least 40 points and Denver has allowed four of the 10 highest point totals in Super Bowl history. However, the Broncos do not hold the record for most turnovers in a Super Bowl nor the most yards allowed in a Super Bowl.

2. Denver has the best winning percentage in conference championship games among those with at least four appearances with an 8-2 mark in AFC Championship Games. Those eight Super Bowl appearances are tied for second most in NFL history with the Dallas Cowboys and Pittsburgh Steelers, trailing only the 11 for the New England Patriots.

3. It's hard to get worse quarterback play in a game than Denver got from its signal-callers in Super Bowl XII. The 35 net passing yards for the Broncos two quarterbacks ranks as the fewest in Super Bowl history and the 32 percent completion percentage is the worst in Super Bowl history. But the play didn't get much better in subsequent Super Bowls. The three worst completion percentages in Super Bowl history belong to Denver quarterbacks with

the Broncos' performance against San Francisco in Super Bowl XXIV and Washington in Super Bowl XXII joining the list.

4. Kicking has also been a woe for the Broncos in Super Bowls. Rich Karlis missed three of his six kicks for the Broncos over the course of two Super Bowls, including a pair of critical misses in the first half of Super Bowl XXI against the Giants that could have extended Denver's lead. Jason Elam also went 2-of-4 on field goals in Denver's win over Atlanta in Super Bowl XXXIII. In all, Broncos kickers are 11-of-16 on field goals in Super Bowls with a long of 51 from Elam in Super Bowl XXXII against Green Bay.

5. The 10-0 lead the Broncos had after the first quarter of Super Bowl XXII against Washington is the largest lead Denver has squandered in a postseason game. The Broncos have led only in two of their five Super Bowl losses and they have trailed in only one of their three Super Bowl victories. In all three of those games, the team that scored first ended up losing the championship that season.

6. Terrell Davis' pivotal second-half performance in Super Bowl XXXII against Green Bay only occurred because of the prolonged halftime. Davis missed the second quarter with a migraine – though some have speculated it might have been a concussion – but the Super Bowl MVP has a history with migraines so he was prepared. He took

medication that takes time to set in, but the extra rest during a Super Bowl halftime allowed the effects to kick in for the second half. Davis went on to rush for 90 of his 157 yards and two of his record three scores after halftime to lift Denver to the upset.

7. With his fourth-quarter touchdown run from 3 yards out against Atlanta, John Elway became the first – and only – quarterback to score at least four career touchdowns in Super Bowls. Elway ran for one touchdown in four of his five Super Bowl appearances and he led the Broncos in rushing in Super Bowl XXI, his first career championship game. In five career Super Bowls, Elway ran for 86 yards on 21 attempts and 4 touchdowns.

8. Super Bowl XLVIII got off to a very poor start for the Broncos as Denver allowed a safety on its first offensive play of the game. Broncos center Manny Ramirez missed Peyton Manning's cadence for the opening snap with Denver pinned deep in its own territory and snapped the ball over Manning's head. Knowshon Moreno fell on the ball for a safety and it was the fastest score in Super Bowl history. After the game, Ramirez told reporters, "It was real loud. We were trying to go on the cadence. I thought I heard him. I didn't. He was actually walking up to me because he had already said the cadence, and I snapped it. But again, I take full responsibility for that."

9. Peyton Manning set several records with Denver's Super Bowl 50 victory despite not having the strongest personal

game. He was the oldest starting quarterback to win the Super Bowl, though that record has been surpassed by Tom Brady, but Manning also earned his 200th win with that championship, breaking a tie with Brett Favre for most combined regular-season and postseason wins in NFL history. Manning is also the only quarterback to win the Super Bowl with two different teams after winning the Super Bowl with the Colts in the 2006 season.

10. Gary Kubiak became the first coach to play for and coach the same franchise in the Super Bowl when he led the Broncos to Super Bowl 50. Kubiak completed all four of his passes in Super Bowl XXI and just one of three in Super Bowl XXIV in his only two Super Bowl appearances as a player. Kubiak is one of five coaches to lead the Broncos to the Super Bowl and joined Mike Shanahan as the only other coach to help Denver win the title.

CHAPTER 10:

DRAFT DAY

QUIZ TIME!

1. Which of these Hall-of-Famers was not drafted by the Broncos while Denver was a member of the AFL?

   a. Dick Butkus

   b. John Mackey

   c. Bob Hayes

   d. Merlin Olsen

2. The Broncos drafted three future Hall-of-Famers in the 1964 AFL Draft, but none of them ever played for the franchise.

   a. True

   b. False

3. Who was the first player from a Colorado-based school drafted by the Broncos?

   a. Chuck Weiss

   b. Sam Strenger

   c. Wayne Lee

   d. Mel Semenko

4. How many times have the Broncos held the No. 1 overall pick in the NFL draft?

   a. 0
   b. 1
   c. 2
   d. 3

5. Which of these Broncos Ring of Fame members was not a first-round pick by the Broncos?

   a. Steve Atwater
   b. Randy Gradishar
   c. Karl Mecklenburg
   d. Louis Wright

6. Denver had five picks in the first two rounds of the 2009 NFL draft. Who was not one of those players selected with one of those choices?

   a. Robert Ayers
   b. Richard Quinn
   c. Alphonso Smith
   d. Zane Beadles

7. Former Broncos quarterback Jake Plummer is the son of Denver's 1969 draft pick Wes Plummer, both of whom played at Arizona State.

   a. True
   b. False

8. In 1973, the Broncos loaded up on key members of their first Super Bowl team in the first four rounds of the draft.

In which round that year did the Broncos draft Tom Jackson?

a. 1st
b. 2nd
c. 3rd
d. 4th

9. Who was not part of that famous 1973 draft class that laid the foundation for Denver's first Super Bowl squad?

a. Paul Howard
b. Riley Odoms
c. Barney Chavous
d. Otis Armstrong

10. With which pick in the first round did Denver draft Dennis Smith in 1981?

a. 10
b. 13
c. 15
d. 19

11. In which round did the Broncos scoop up running back Sammy Winder out of Southern Mississippi in the 1982 NFL draft?

a. 3rd
b. 4th
c. 5th
d. 7th

12. Which future NFL head coach was Denver's eighth-round pick in 1983?

    a. Gary Kubiak
    b. Andy Reid
    c. Mike Mularkey
    d. Jeff Fisher

13. In which round did the Broncos take a flyer on Marlin Briscoe in the 1968 NFL draft?

    a. 12th
    b. 14th
    c. 16th
    d. 18th

14. People have become obsessed with some of the more unusual names in the NFL draft each year. Which one of these players was not drafted by the Broncos?

    a. Fritz Fequiere
    b. Le-Lo Lang
    c. Butler B'ynot'e
    d. Dietrich Lockridge

15. In which year did Denver wisely use a third-round pick on kicker Jason Elam out of Hawaii?

    a. 1995
    b. 1994
    c. 1993
    d. 1992

16. The Broncos drafted Demaryius Thomas and Tim Tebow in the same first round.

    a. True
    b. False

17. In which round of the 2012 NFL draft did Denver select Danny Trevathan?

    a. 4th
    b. 5th
    c. 6th
    d. 7th

18. How many times have the Broncos drafted a quarterback in the first round?

    a. 3
    b. 4
    c. 5
    d. 6

19. The Broncos have never drafted an offensive player in the top five of the NFL draft.

    a. True
    b. False

20. When was the last time Denver did not have a first-round pick?

    a. 2010
    b. 2011
    c. 2012
    d. 2013

QUIZ ANSWERS

1. B – John Mackey

2. A – True

3. D – Mel Semenko

4. A – 0

5. C – Karl Mecklenburg

6. D – Zane Beadles

7. B – False

8. D – 4th

9. B – Riley Odoms

10. C – 15

11. C – 5th

12. A – Gary Kubiak

13. B – 14th

14. It's a trick question. All of these players were drafted by Denver in the 1990s.

15. C – 1993

16. A – True

17. C – 6th

18. B – 4

19. B – False

20. C – 2012

DID YOU KNOW?

1. Lyle Alzado wasn't on many teams' radars coming out of Yankton College in South Dakota for the 1971 NFL draft. He certainly wasn't on anyone's mind in Denver until a fortunate misfortune for a Broncos scout in Montana. The scout's car broke down and he asked Montana Tech for some film to watch while the car was being repaired. He saw Alzado's dominance along the defensive line and the Broncos ended up drafting Alzado in the fourth round in 1971. Alzado made 98 starts in eight seasons for Denver and was a two-time Pro Bowler while helping the Broncos reach the Super Bowl in 1977.

2. Chris Hinton will always be known as the offensive lineman traded for John Elway after Denver drafted him with the fourth overall pick in the 1983 draft. Hinton had an excellent career in his own right after the trade that would come to define his career. He was selected for seven Pro Bowls, including the 1983 edition, when he became the first rookie offensive lineman to start the All-Star game. He played 13 seasons in the league and was named a First Team All-Pro twice and a second-teamer three other times.

3. Hinton also played a role in bringing Karl Mecklenburg to the Broncos' attention for the 1983 draft. While Denver was watching film of Hinton's Northwestern team

playing against Minnesota, they noticed that Mecklenburg beat Hinton twice for two sacks. It took a while for the Broncos to actually pull the trigger on Mecklenburg, drafting him 310th overall in the 12th round, but he became a staple at linebacker for Denver for 12 seasons. Mecklenburg was perhaps naïve about his chances of making the team as a late-round pick, but he told ESPN, "I felt like I was going to make it right from the start. ... I was overconfident and foolish. I never lacked for confidence in my own ability. It was just a matter of getting the opportunity."

4. Perhaps it was fortunate for Randy Gradishar that there wasn't a scouting combine in 1974 when he was coming out of Ohio State. Most teams relied on their own scouting and medical exams, but it became a well-known secret that Gradishar had failed his physical for two teams after suffering numerous injuries in college. John Ralston, Denver's coach and general manager at the time, knew Gradishar would fit his team-first defense and was undeterred by the injury history. Put simply by Ralston after the Broncos made Gradishar the 14th pick in the draft that year, "Gradishar was not a player you could pass up."

5. It's going to take a lot for John Elway to surpass his first-ever draft as Broncos general manager. After taking over the reins of the Broncos in 2011, Elway selected Von Miller with the second overall pick in the draft. Miller is on his way to a Hall of Fame career, but Elway also added

several other valuable pieces in the 2011 NFL draft. Three other players started in Super Bowl XLVIII against Seattle and a fourth was slated to start but missed the game due to injury.

6. Elway was so set on drafting Bradley Chubb at No. 5 overall in 2018 that he was ready to trade the pick to the Buffalo Bills had Chubb not been there. The proposed deal was Denver's fifth pick and a third-round selection in 2018 for Buffalo's two first-round picks (Nos. 12 and 22) and a second-round selection that year. It is unknown which third-round pick Elway was going to part with, but he ended up keeping the picks and drafting running back Royce Freeman and cornerback Isaac Yiadom.

7. The Broncos didn't have a first-round draft pick twice in the last 20 years – in 2005 and 2012 – and both times they held the 25th pick in the draft. Washington traded with Denver in 2005 in exchange for a 2005 third-rounder, a 2006 first-rounder that the Broncos traded to San Francisco, a third-round selection in 2006, and the 2006 fourth-round pick that Denver used to draft receiver Brandon Marshall. In 2012, Denver traded with the Patriots to drop down to No. 31, but then they flipped that 31st pick to Tampa Bay for the second-round pick the Broncos used to draft Derek Wolfe and a fourth-round selection they used on Omar Bolden.

8. Shannon Sharpe is never shy on confidence and that was even true when it came to his draft experience in 1990.

The receiver out of Savannah State just assumed he was going to be a first-round pick. When he wasn't selected, he thought he wouldn't slip past the third round. By the time the 12-round draft took a break after the sixth round, Sharpe admitted to ESPN he was in shock that he was still available. The following morning, he went to work out with his brother, Sterling, in their hometown of Glenville, Georgia, and he returned home to a phone call from a Broncos scout letting him know Denver had drafted him in the seventh round.

9. Terrell Davis actually victimized the Green Bay Packers in two ways during Super Bowl XXXII. He not only ran all over the Packers to help Denver win its first championship, but he also showed them what they missed out on by not drafting him in 1995. Green Bay's general manager at the time, Ron Wolf, told Gil Brandt that the biggest regret of his tenure in Green Bay was not drafting Terrell Davis in 1995. During that draft, a young Packers scout continued to go to bat for the Packers to pick Davis, but he was largely ignored. That scout turned out to be John Dorsey, who went on to become Cleveland's general manager.

10. Denver has had some success with its late-round picks throughout its history. Among those who outperformed their draft stock were 2006 fourth-round pick Elvis Dumervil, 2000 sixth-round draftee Mike Anderson, and seventh-rounder Peyton Hillis. But perhaps none of them did better than Tom Nalen, whom Denver drafted in the

seventh round of the 1994 NFL draft. The Broncos received 188 games of service and an anchor of the offensive line from a seventh-rounder and, although he isn't in the Hall of Fame, he might be the biggest steal the Broncos have had in a draft.

CHAPTER 11:

LET'S MAKE A DEAL

QUIZ TIME!

1. Which future Hall-of-Famer did the Broncos ship off to the Kansas City Chiefs for a fourth-round pick due to a position dispute after drafting him in the second round?

   a. Dick Butkus

   b. Merlin Olsen

   c. Curley Culp

   d. Bob Brown

2. Which player did the Broncos send to Dallas to acquire Austin "Goose" Gonsoulin in 1960?

   a. Jack Spikes

   b. Luther Hayes

   c. Gordy Holz

   d. Bob Scarpitto

3. Who was the defensive tackle the Broncos received when they shipped Willie Brown and Mickey Slaughter to Oakland in 1967?

a. Bill Keating

b. Dave Costa

c. Jerry Inman

d. Rex Mirich

4. How many first-round picks did the Broncos send to San Diego in their trade for Steve Tensi?

    a. 0

    b. 1

    c. 2

    d. 3

5. After trading for both Abner Hayes and Cookie Gilchrist in 1965, Denver later packaged Hayes as part of a deal that brought Gilchrist back to the Broncos two years later.

    a. True

    b. False

6. From which team did the Broncos acquire Haven Moses in 1972?

    a. San Diego Chargers

    b. Buffalo Bills

    c. Chicago Bears

    d. New England Patriots

7. Denver sent Richard Jackson to Cleveland in 1972 in exchange for a third-round pick that the Broncos used to draft which offensive lineman?

    a. Paul Howard

    b. Claudie Minor

c. Tom Glassic

d. Jerome Kundich

8. In which round was the pick Denver sent with Steve Ramsey to the New York Giants in exchange for Craig Morton?

    a. 3rd

    b. 4th

    c. 5th

    d. 6th

9. The third-rounder the Broncos acquired when trading Lyle Alzado to the Oakland Raiders was used to draft Rulon Jones.

    a. True

    b. False

10. The Broncos used the second-round selection they acquired from Tampa Bay in the Steve DeBerg trade to move up in the second round of the 1985 NFL draft to draft Vance Johnson.

    a. True

    b. False

11. In which round was the draft pick Denver sent Dallas as part of the Tony Dorsett deal?

    a. 4th

    b. 5th

    c. 6th

    d. 8th

12. Which team wanted to move up in the first round of the 1989 NFL draft and swapped first-round picks with Denver, ultimately leading to the Broncos drafting Steve Atwater?

    a. Green Bay Packers

    b. Cincinnati Bengals

    c. New York Jets

    d. Cleveland Browns

13. Which draft pick did Denver not send to Minnesota as part of the Gary Zimmerman trade?

    a. 1st Round 1994

    b. 1st Round 1995

    c. 2nd Round 1995

    d. 6th Round 1994

14. Who was the player sent to the New York Giants for the seventh-round pick that Denver used to draft Tom Nalen?

    a. Tommy Maddox

    b. Alton Montgomery

    c. Arthur Marshall

    d. Bobby Humphrey

15. Which of these players was not selected with a pick Denver acquired by trading down in the draft?

    a. Dan Neil

    b. Deltha O'Neal

    c. Terrell Davis

    d. Brandon Marshall

16. Which draft pick did the Broncos not acquire by trading out of the first round in 2005 in a deal with Washington?

a. 1st Round 2006

b. 2nd Round 2006

c. 3rd Round 2005

d. 3rd Round 2006

17. The Broncos traded a first-round pick in the 2006 draft three times before selecting Jay Cutler.

a. True

b. False

18. To which team did Denver trade Jake Plummer in 2007?

a. Arizona Cardinals

b. Baltimore Ravens

c. Tampa Bay Buccaneers

d. New York Jets

19. What two draft picks went to San Francisco in the trade to acquire Vernon Davis?

a. 5th Round 2015 and 6th Round 2016

b. 5th Round 2016 and 5th Round 2017

c. 5th Round 2016 and 6th Round 2017

d. 6th Round 2016 and 6th Round 2017

20. Who was Denver's trading partner when it moved up in the 2019 NFL draft to select Drew Lock in the second round?

a. Buffalo Bills

b. Minnesota Vikings

c. Cincinnati Bengals

d. New England Patriots

QUIZ ANSWERS

1. C – Curley Culp

2. A – Jack Spikes

3. D – Rex Mirich

4. C – 2

5. A – True

6. B – Buffalo Bills

7. A – Paul Howard

8. C – 5th

9. B – False

10. A – True

11. B – 5th

12. D – Cleveland Browns

13. B – 1st Round 1994

14. C – Arthur Marshall

15. A – Dan Neill

16. B – 2nd Round 2006

17. A – True

18. C – Tampa Bay Buccaneers

19. D – 6th Round 2016 and 6th Round 2017

20. C – Cincinnati Bengals

DID YOU KNOW?

1. One of the biggest missteps in Broncos history was trading Hall-of-Famer Curley Culp to a division rival before he even took a snap for Denver. The Broncos had drafted Culp as an offensive lineman, but Culp wanted to play defensive tackle. When the situation became untenable, the Broncos shipped Culp to the Chiefs and he blossomed into a disruptive force in the middle of Hank Stram's 3-4 defense. His play at nose tackle helped the Chiefs beat Minnesota in Super Bowl IV and he made four straight Pro Bowls under Bum Phillips in Houston.

2. The Broncos made two trades with the rival Oakland Raiders in 1967, dealing two of Denver's brightest stars to Oakland. The first trade sent future Hall of Fame cornerback Willie Brown and quarterback Mickey Slaughter to Oakland for defensive lineman Rex Mirich and a third-round draft pick. The trade is immortalized in the Pro Football Hall of Fame, which has the original telegram Raiders owner Al Davis sent to Lou Saban confirming the details of the trade. Later that year, the Broncos shipped Lionel Taylor, the team's first star receiver, to Oakland with center Jerry Strum for three players, including defensive lineman Rich Jackson.

3. Denver's first trade as a franchise brought in one of the best Broncos to ever suit up in the orange and blue to

town. The Broncos sent fullback Jack Spikes to the Dallas Texans for Austin "Goose" Gonsoulin in the quiet aftermath of the 1960 AFL draft. Gonsoulin became part of the first class to be inducted into the Broncos' Ring of Fame and he still holds several team records. A native of Texas who played his college football at Baylor, he once said about the trade to Denver, "I knew Denver was in the West, but that was about the extent of my awareness. I had to check some maps to see exactly where I was going. It was my first time to spend a significant period away from the state of Texas."

4. One of Denver's most underrated trades was when they flipped kickers with the New York Jets in 1971. The Broncos sent Bobby Howfield to New York and acquired Jim Turner, who went on to play a crucial role in the Broncos' playoff success over the next decade. Turner once said the swirling winds in Shea Stadium helped prepare him for kicking in the Denver weather. He retired as Denver's all-time leading scorer with 742 points over nine seasons with the Broncos, and he also retired as the second-leading scorer all-time in the NFL.

5. The Broncos took a risk in 1988 when they traded a fifth-round pick in the 1989 draft to Dallas in exchange for Tony Dorsett. Denver hoped that a new environment and a reunion with Dan Reeves would revitalize Dorsett's career after a rough 1987 season. According to an article in *Sports Illustrated* ahead of the 1988 season, Dorsett had run a 4.38 40-yard dash in Denver and was looking like his

speedy self. Dorsett led the Broncos in rushing in 1988 but he had just 703 yards and 5 touchdowns before retiring before the 1989 season after tearing his ACL.

6. As surprising as it sounds, the Broncos didn't fully reject an offer for John Elway in 1991. In a radio interview in 2017, former Washington general manager Charley Casserly said he once inquired about how much it would cost for Washington to trade for Elway. The Broncos didn't say no at first and came back the following day to say that any deal would be centered on Washington's three-time All-Pro tackle Jim Lachey. Washington rejected that notion and the following day, Denver said it had no plans to move on from Elway as its quarterback.

7. Two years after using a first-round pick to draft Tommy Maddox, the Broncos were very close to cutting him for salary cap concerns. Maddox refused a pay cut to stay in Denver as Elway's backup and instead the Broncos traded him to the Rams for a fourth-round pick in the 1995 draft. There was some discussion about the draft pick the Rams were going to send to the Broncos with Denver asking for a third and Los Angeles countering with a fifth-round selection before compromising in the middle.

8. Many people blame the Jay Cutler trade on setting back the Broncos for almost a decade, but the quarterback didn't really give the team much of a choice. Cutler was unhappy with new coach Josh McDaniels and he did not report to offseason training programs nor did he respond

to communications with McDaniels or owner Pat Bowlen. Cutler and his agent, Bus Cook, disputed the claims that Cutler had been ignoring him, but the bad blood between the two sides reached a crescendo before the 2009 NFL draft. Denver traded their potential franchise quarterback to Chicago for Kyle Orton and a first-round pick in both 2009 and 2010 as well as a third-rounder in 2009.

9. Sometimes the stories behind the trades not made are even funnier than the ones behind the deals actually completed. Around the 2015 NFL trade deadline, Broncos quarterback Peyton Manning reached out to Browns left tackle Joe Thomas about trying to force a trade for the Pro Bowler to Denver. According to Thomas, Manning was persistent in trying to pester Thomas into demanding a trade, even at one point suggesting that Thomas defile the general manager's desk in Cleveland. Obviously, the deal never came close to being completed, but it was a funny story that Thomas can one day tell people about his career.

10. Denver has a rich history of trading for starting quarterbacks as opposed to drafting them itself. The list of starting quarterbacks the Broncos have traded for includes Joe Flacco in 2018, Kyle Orton in 2009, Craig Morton in 1977, and Steve Tensi in 1967. However, Denver also has a history of flipping quarterbacks in the trade market for good value. The sixth-round pick Denver used to draft Danny Trevathan came in the Tim Tebow trade, the seventh-rounder used to select Peyton Hillis

came from the Jake Plummer trade, and, six years after trading for Steve Ramsey, Denver sent him to New York in the deal to acquire Craig Morton.

CHAPTER 12:

WRITING THE RECORD BOOK

QUIZ TIME!

1. John Elway set the record for most passing yards in a game by a rookie quarterback against which fitting opponent?

    a. Oakland Raiders
    b. Kansas City Chiefs
    c. Baltimore Colts
    d. San Diego Chargers

2. John Elway also holds the team record for most interceptions thrown by a large margin. How many interceptions did he throw during his career?

    a. 193
    b. 201
    c. 212
    d. 226

3. Both the warmest and coldest games in Broncos history were played in Denver.

a. True

b. False

4. What is the most points the Broncos have scored at home since 2001, when the new Mile High Stadium was opened?

   a. 49

   b. 52

   c. 56

   d. 64

5. Which quarterback threw for a team-record 499 yards in a loss to Atlanta?

   a. Jake Plummer

   b. Peyton Manning

   c. Jay Cutler

   d. Kyle Orton

6. Which former Denver quarterback holds the franchise record for most consecutive passes without throwing an interception?

   a. Peyton Manning

   b. John Elway

   c. Trevor Siemian

   d. Jake Plummer

7. Which former Broncos running back holds the NFL record for most yards gained (receiving, rushing, and returns) in a game?

   a. Floyd Little

   b. Rick Upchurch

c. Terrell Davis

d. Glyn Milburn

8. The 2013 Denver offense set several NFL records while tearing through the league en route to the Super Bowl. Which of these NFL records do those Broncos not hold at this time?

a. Most total yards in a season

b. Most points in a season

c. Most passing yards in a season

d. Most touchdowns in a season

9. Which Broncos backup holds the record for best completion percentage in a playoff game with a minimum of 12 throws?

a. Norm Weese

b. Steve DeBerg

c. Gary Kubiak

d. Tommy Maddox

10. Lance Alworth holds the record for most receiving yards against the Broncos with 211 yards in a 1965 game.

a. True

b. False

11. Which running back tore up the Denver defense for 278 yards to set the record for most rushing yards against the Broncos in a single game?

a. Corey Dillon

b. Jamaal Charles

c. Larry Johnson

d. LaDainian Tomlinson

12. Which quarterback is the only player to complete 40 passes against a Denver defense, doing it twice just three years apart?

a. Ben Roethlisberger

b. Jim Kelly

c. Tom Brady

d. Drew Brees

13. Which team was the victim of the largest shutout victory by the Broncos in their history, a 37-0 blanking back in 1989?

a. Seattle Seahawks

b. Minnesota Vikings

c. Los Angeles Rams

d. Phoenix Cardinals

14. Terrell Davis is the Broncos all-time leader in playoff scoring with 84 points on 14 touchdowns scored.

a. True

b. False

15. What is the most plays Denver has ever run in a non-overtime game?

a. 83

b. 87

c. 91

d. 95

16. Jason Elam holds the Broncos record with a 99.5% conversion rate on extra points. How many did he miss in his Denver career?

   a. 1
   b. 2
   c. 3
   d. 4

17. In which two seasons did Jason Elam set the record for most field goals made in a season with 31?

   a. 1994 and 1995
   b. 1995 and 2001
   c. 1994 and 1999
   d. 2001 and 2004

18. Who holds the record for most career punts for the Denver franchise?

   a. Mike Horan
   b. Britton Colquitt
   c. Tom Rouen
   d. Bill Van Heusen

19. Trindon Holliday is the only Broncos player to have a kickoff return touchdown in two different seasons. What was identical about his record-tying two kickoff return scores?

   a. They both were Denver's first points of the game.
   b. They were against the same opponent.
   c. They both were the opening kickoff of a half.
   d. They were the same length.

20. The Broncos have a winning record as a franchise.

    a. True
    b. False

QUIZ ANSWERS

1. C – Baltimore Colts

2. D – 226

3. B – False

4. B – 52

5. A – Jake Plummer

6. D – Jake Plummer

7. D – Glyn Milburn

8. A – Most total yards in a season

9. C – Gary Kubiak

10. B – False

11. A – Corey Dillon

12. A – Ben Roethlisberger

13. D – Phoenix Cardinals

14. B – False

15. C – 91

16. C – 3

17. B – 1995 & 2001

18. C – Tom Rouen

19. D – They were the same length.

20. A – True

DID YOU KNOW?

1. On January 12, 1992, Gary Kubiak had a chance to be the hero for the Broncos. John Elway left the AFC Championship Game against Buffalo with a thigh injury, so Kubiak had to play the entire fourth quarter. He completed 11 of his 12 passes in the quarter to rally the Broncos against a stout Bills defense and scored a 3-yard rushing touchdown for Denver's only points. Kubiak's 91.7 percent completion percentage is the highest single-game total in Broncos history and his 84.2 completion percentage in all postseason appearances leads the franchise as well.

2. December 10, 1995, was a special day to watch Glyn Milburn do what he does best. Despite Denver losing to Seattle 31-27 that day, Milburn ran for 131 yards on 18 carries, caught 5 passes for 45 yards, returned 5 kickoffs for 133 yards, and added 95 yards on 5 punt returns. The total was 404 yards, an NFL record and the Broncos record for total yards in a game by almost 110 yards. That contest was the only 100-yard rushing game of Milburn's career and he never ran for more than 54 yards in any other game.

3. The two greatest rushing performances by total yards in Broncos history were accomplished by rookie running backs. In 2000, Mike Anderson gashed the New Orleans Saints for 251 yards and four touchdowns on just 37

carries to set the franchise record. Just two seasons later, Clinton Portis closed his first season in the league by running for 228 yards and two late touchdowns against Arizona. The two running backs had very similar first seasons and rank first and second in many of the key rookie rushing statistics in the record books. They are first and second in yards and both share the record with 15 rushing scores as a rookie.

4. Jake Plummer's franchise-record passing day did not come in a winning effort, and it wasn't particularly close. While Plummer did throw for 499 yards in a Week 8 game with Atlanta in 2004, the Falcons won that game by 13 points, largely due to Plummer's 3 interceptions, which almost washed out his 4 passing touchdowns. The 55 attempts Plummer had in the loss is only the eighth most by a Broncos quarterback. It was largely uncharacteristic for Plummer, who holds the Broncos record for most consecutive passes with out an interception at 229 and has the second best winning percentage of any Denver quarterback.

5. Continuing the trend of having a record-setting day in a losing effort, Brandon Marshall's NFL record 21 catches in a game came in a Denver loss to Indianapolis. Marshall was targeted 28 times in that game and he caught 21 of Kyle Orton's 29 completions in what was his only 200-yard game as a member of the Broncos. He caught both of Denver's touchdowns in the game and accounted for just 20 fewer passing yards than Peyton Manning had for the

Colts that day. It took only 8 catches for Demaryius Thomas to set the receiving yards record with 226 yards in a win over Arizona.

6. Simon Fletcher turned up his play a notch or five after Denver's bye week in Week 9 of the 1992 season. Fletcher had just 3.5 sacks in the first nine games of the season, but then he went on a tear in the final seven games that bled into the 1993 campaign. He had a sack in every one of those seven games, totaling 12.5 sacks total to set the Broncos record – since broken – at 16 sacks. Fletcher then had a sack in each of the first three games of 1993, tying the NFL record of 10 consecutive games with a sack. He had four multi-sack games during the streak – all in 1992 – and the 15.5 sacks he had in the streak would have been the fourth-best single-season total in franchise history.

7. The 2013 Broncos offense, led by Peyton Manning, was basically unstoppable during the regular season. The unit holds the top three single-game point totals and three of the four 50-point performances in franchise history. One of those games wasn't Oct. 27, when the Broncos set the record for most points in a quarter – 31 in the fourth – and most points in a half --- 38 in the second – in a come-from-behind win over Washington. Despite holding the team record for total yards in a season and average gain per play, the 2013 squad fell 16 yards shy of the record for most yards in a game, a record Denver topped the following year.

8. On three separate occasions, the Broncos have overcome a 24-point deficit in the third quarter to win games. It happened the first time on October 23, 1960, when Denver scored 31 straight points to beat the Patriots after falling behind 24-0. On September 23, 1979, the Broncos scored 27 consecutive points to nip Seattle 37-34; then, on October 15, 2012, Denver scored five unanswered touchdowns to overcome a 24-0 deficit to the Chargers. The 24-point margin is also the largest lead the Broncos have squandered, though both those losses came in overtime. Denver led the Raiders 24-0 late in the first half on September 26, 1988, before losing 30-27 in overtime. On November 24, 2013, Denver took a 24-0 lead midway through the second quarter in New England, only to lose 34-31 in overtime.

9. When it comes to extreme weather, Kansas City in mid-December is the place for the Broncos. The coldest game in franchise history was played December 18, 1983, at Arrowhead Stadium, with an official game temperature of 0 degrees and a wind chill of 30 below. The coldest game in Denver was a 1972 contest against San Diego with a recorded temperature of 9 degrees, tying for second with another game in Kansas City. In fact, all three games the Broncos have played with a negative wind chill have come at the Chiefs' home field. All three of Denver's warmest games also came on the road with a high of 103 degrees in Arizona on September 23, 2001. By contrast, it was a balmy 92 degrees in Denver on September 16, 2018, for the warmest game in the Mile High City.

10. Since the AFL-NFL merger in 1970, the Broncos have at least a .500 record against all four of their division rivals. Denver technically has a record of 54-65 against Kansas City, but since joining the NFL the Broncos lead the overall series with the Chiefs, 53-46. The Broncos are 67-52-1 against the Chargers overall, but that is largely due to a 62-37-1 advantage since the merger. Denver has just 53 wins against the Raiders compared to 64 losses and two ties in the teams' history, but they are an even 49-49-1 since 1970. Denver also had a 32-17 record against the Seahawks over the 25 seasons Seattle played in the AFC West.

CONCLUSION

If we've done our job correctly, you've learned a lot of new facts about your favorite NFL team, the Denver Broncos. Whether it's which notable players still hold franchise records or some of the behind-the-scenes information about how some of your favorite players became who they are, we hope you enjoyed this trip through Broncos history. We tried to cover it all from the joys of winning three Super Bowls to some of the dark days in the franchise's history.

Over the last four decades, Denver has been one of the best franchises in the NFL, with eight Super Bowl appearances and 29 winning seasons in its history. Some of the best players in the history of the sport have called Denver home, including the great John Elway, who is making a name for himself as an executive as well. The Broncos might not be as well-represented in the Hall of Fame as fans would hope, but we hope we at least gave justice to the great Broncos of the past and present.

This book is designed for you, the fans, to be able to embrace your favorite team and feel closer to them. Maybe you weren't familiar with the history of the franchise or were unaware of how well the Broncos chose players in the AFL draft. Perhaps you weren't aware of the trades that led to Denver drafting franchise-changing talent. Or maybe we couldn't stump you at all and you're the ultimate superfan. No matter how well you did on the quizzes, we hope we captured the spirit of the Broncos and injected you with even more pride for your team.

The future is again bright for the Broncos with a young quarterback, a future Hall of Fame linebacker, and an executive committed to keeping Denver as one of the top destinations in the NFL. This franchise has come a long way from almost moving out of Denver and is now entrenched in the fabric of the city. The Broncos are a staple in the NFL now and will always be one of the most respected franchises in the league, so fans should be excited about what the future holds for this team.